PRODUCT MANAGEMENT AND STRATEGY

The Ultimate Guide that Creates Real Value

GAGANDEEP SINGH

INDIA • SINGAPORE • MALAYSIA

Notion Press

No.8, 3rd Cross Street
CIT Colony, Mylapore
Chennai, Tamil Nadu – 600004

First Published by Notion Press 2021
Copyright © Gagandeep Singh 2021
All Rights Reserved.

ISBN

Hardcase: 978-1-63745-475-6
Paperback: 978-1-63745-476-3

This book has been published with all efforts taken to make the material error-free after the consent of the author. However, the author and the publisher do not assume and hereby disclaim any liability to any party for any loss, damage, or disruption caused by errors or omissions, whether such errors or omissions result from negligence, accident, or any other cause.

While every effort has been made to avoid any mistake or omission, this publication is being sold on the condition and understanding that neither the author nor the publishers or printers would be liable in any manner to any person by reason of any mistake or omission in this publication or for any action taken or omitted to be taken or advice rendered or accepted on the basis of this work. For any defect in printing or binding the publishers will be liable only to replace the defective copy by another copy of this work then available.

Contents

Magic of Numbers 5

Privacy Really Matters 23

Thinking Strategically 33

Building the Right Product 49

Creating Business Case 63

Build a Brand 73

References *83*

Magic of Numbers

If you are into product management and always thinking about presenting a strong business case with the right set of numbers in place, so that the product idea is marketable to stakeholders, then you are on the right track. However, the question that comes up is – Do I need to understand the curiosity of my finance team? Why will they sponsor this project? Is my company financially liberal to sponsor a product idea or are there any liquidity constraints due to which I should pitch the product idea later?

Some executives working on product management or product strategy, face such concerns regularly from their stakeholders.

"Do you have a strong business case?"

"Do you think this is viable, does it make any business sense?"

"There is a fixed cost to this project, how will you measure the ROI?"

"It is good at an innovation level but will not bring in revenue for the business."

"We are running healthy products, why is the organization spending money on their ideas?"

"Organizations should focus on the current Box 1 strategy (managing the present). Why are they spending on the Box 3 strategy (creating the future)?"

When answering the questions mentioned above, it is essential to communicate in the language of finance, i.e., with numbers. So, let's take the discussion ahead with how the magic of numbers works and makes your life simpler, instilling more confidence.

It is most important to understand the magic of numbers, if you want to go up the organization's ladder. At a certain level, you will find your companions talking about the organization's financial health or hear them discuss how certain products are not doing financially well. There might be dialogue on the need to make a cost reduction in specific products since they are facing multiple financial constraints. They may talk about controlling the budget properly in order to show a reasonable profit to the business. Thus, to be more participative in such discussions and not feel left out, it is of utmost importance that you are conversing in a similar language.

Then, the question comes up – Do these numbers bother you if you are in software development, marketing, product development, compliance, legal, data privacy, corporate communications, etc.? The answer is a big 'YES'. Some elements of these numbers have a direct or indirect impact on your department. Therefore, understanding these will make you more assertive, giving you the knowledge of where the organization is heading and when to ask for more resources (human or inventory, etc.) or pitch yourself in for a due promotion.

U.S. Securities and Exchange Commission says, "If you can read a nutrition label or a baseball box score, you can learn to read basic financial statements. If you can follow a recipe or apply for a loan, you can learn basic accounting. The basics are not complicated and are not rocket science."

Financial Statements

Let's find out where the money is. However, before we proceed, I am reminded of a fascinating dialogue from the Indian movie, Bazaar, which says - "Paisa Uska Joh Dhanda Jaanta ho," i.e., "**Money belongs to the one who knows about the business.**" So, let's start the business.

There are four financial statements that a company prepares:

1. Balance Sheet
2. Income Statement
3. Cash Flow Statement
4. Owner's/Stakeholder's Equity Statement

The balance sheet shows what your company owns and what it owes at a fixed point in time. The income statement reflects how much money a company made and spent over a period. The cash flow statement shows the exchange of money between a company and the outside world, also over a period. The fourth financial statement called the 'Stakeholder Equity Statement', shows changes in the interests of the company's shareholders over time.

Balance Sheet

The balance sheet reports the **assets** (what the company owns), **liabilities** (what the company owes) and the **Owner's/Shareholder's equity** (book value or net worth) at a given point in time. It also refers to the statement of the financial position of a company at a given point in time.

Assets

Assets are the resources which the business owns. They are classified as current or fixed assets, and have the economic value to provide future services or benefits.

Current Assets are those assets that can be liquidated within one year, such as cash and equivalents, marketable securities, accounts receivable, prepaid expenses and any other liquid assets.

Fixed Assets (Non-Current Assets) are long-term assets that have a useful life of over one year, such as property, plant and equipment, investments, intangible assets and any other long-term assets.

Assets also include certain elements such as trademarks, patents, copyrights, domain names and brand names, which cannot be touched. They, however, exist and have value. These assets are known as **Intangible Assets**.

As a product manager, you would have been contributing to many of these intangible assets such as trademark of the product when you plan to launch your product in multiple countries, control of domain names or patent some of the frameworks as a part of the product platform strategy, so that your idea/research and development effort remains yours. If you don't do this strategically, it might incur extra costs during the buyout and will lead to a higher expense on your balance sheet.

Let's go through the specific elements of Trademark/Patent and Goodwill, which is an area of interest for most product managers.

- **Trademark and Patent**

    Trademarks and Patents are captured as intangible assets under the balance sheet. Trademarks are the logos, symbols, designs, words, phrases, symbols, or a combination of all, for which the company is registered under the specific jurisdiction, where the business operates or is planning to operate. It recognises and differentiates the services of one company or party from those of another. For accounting, Trademark is capitalised, which means it is recorded in the books of accounts as an asset through a journal entry.

- **Goodwill**

    Goodwill (established reputation of business) is also an intangible asset that comes in place due to a merger and acquisition. It records when a company acquires another company and the purchase price is higher than its asset's fair market value. The difference in the cost refers to as goodwill. For example, company ABC acquires another company XYZ, at 10 million USD. Company XYZ has assets of 9 million USD, and liabilities of 1 million USD, so the fair value is nine minus one, i.e., 8. Here the company ABC has paid 2 million USD as goodwill.

There is a test called the **Impairment Test**, which should be conducted every year to determine whether the asset's economic benefit has dropped. If the investor has paid more than the fair value, it means there is a probability to generate enough profits through new business, thus providing satisfactory returns. However, whether the new investment is making adequate returns or overstated or is the value worth, will be determined through the annual test of impairment.

Liabilities

A Liability is the amount of money that a company owes to others. It could be your suppliers or other creditors. They are categorised as current liabilities and long-term liabilities.

Current liabilities are the payment obligations that are due within a year. They require the use of the current assets or may create another current liability. They include accounts/trade payable, income taxes payable, interest payable, wages payable, due to banks (current repayment obligation on a long-term loan), other expenses payable, etc.

Long-term liabilities are the liabilities that are not due within one year of the balance sheet's date. They include finance liabilities, lease liabilities, deferred income taxes, deferred revenues, etc. They are also known as Non-Current Liabilities.

Owner's/Shareholder's Equity

It is defined as money left when a company has sold all its assets and paid off all its liabilities. This leftover money belongs to the owner (proprietorship firm) or the shareholders/stockholders (in case of a corporation). There is one modest distinction between shareholder equity and net worth. When the discussion is about net worth, it reflects on an individual entity and signifies a firm when it is about shareholder equity. Shareholder's equity includes Contributed Capital (or paid-in Capital), preference share capital and retained earnings.

If a firm has total assets of 100,000 USD and liabilities of 50,000 USD, the shareholder's equity would be 50,000 USD.

Share Capital, Paid-in Capital, Equity Capital, Contributed Capital

- **Share Capital**

    Share Capital is the fundraising by the institutions from the issue of their common shares from public and private sources. It is shown under owner's equity, on the liability side of the balance sheet.

- **Paid-in Capital**

    Paid-in Capital is the money the organization receives in exchange for the shares sold in the primary market, i.e., shares sold directly to the investors by the issuer. These shares are not in the secondary market, where investors sell their shares to other investors and can have the two **common** and **preferred** stock. Paid-in Capital is part of the subscribed share capital.

    Paid-in Capital = Common Stock + Additional Paid-in Capital (APIC)

- **Contributed Capital**

    Contributed Capital is the equity investment accorded by the shareholders/investors in a company. It is the amount of cash and other assets that shareholders/investors have given to the company in exchange for stocks. Secondly, when the buyers buy the shares from the open market, the amount of shares is directly received by the investors selling them.

Retained Earnings

Retained earnings are business profits, which can be used for investing back in the business for working capital needs, fixed asset purchases or reducing debts. These earnings are not distributed as dividends to its shareholders.

Accounting Equation

The accounting equation is the basic principle of accounting and is defined as:

Total Assets = Total Liabilities + Owner's/Shareholders Equity.

The Equity Expanded accounting equation for a corporation is defined as:

Expanded accounting equation = Paid-Up Capital – Treasury Stock (if any) + Liabilities + Income – Expenses – Dividends

Example of a Balance Sheet

We will be taking an example of an imaginary company, say ABC, for understanding the financial structure of its balance sheet, income statement and cash flow.

ABC Corporation					
Balance Sheet					
December 31, 2019					
			2019	2018	Increase (Decrease)
Assets					
Current assets					
		Cash & cash equivalents	100,000	75,000	25,000
		Marketable Securities	50,000	40,000	10,000
		Accounts Receivable	25,000	21,000	4,000
		Inventories	40,000	38,000	2,000
		Prepaid Expenses	20,000	15,000	5,000
			Total Current Assets	235,000	189,000	46,000
Fixed assets					
		Property, plant & equipment	500,000	400,000	100,000

Continued…

		Long term investments		100,000	85,000	15,000
		Total Fixed assets		600,000	485,000	115,000
Intangible assets						
		Goodwill		30,000	25,000	5,000
		Tradename		25,000	20,000	5,000
		Total Intangible assets		55,000	45,000	10,000
		Total assets		890,000	719,000	171,000
Liabilities and Stakeholders Equity						
Current Liabilities						
		Accounts payable		45,000	41,000	4,000
		Income taxes payable		18,000	10,000	8,000
		Wages payable		50,000	40,000	10,000
		Interest payable (short term debt)		60,000	62,000	(2,000)
		Accrued expense		49,000	32,000	17,000
			Total Current Liabilities	222,000	185,000	37,000
Long Term Liabilities						
		Long term debt		210,000	180,000	30,000
		Total Liabilities		432,000	365,000	67,000

Shareholders' Equity						
	Contributed capital			350,000	280,000	70,000
	Retained earnings			108,000	74,000	34,000
		Total owner's equity		458,000	354,000	104,000
		Total liabilities and owner's equity		890,000	719,000	171,000

It's always good to know how your company numbers are progressing and how your contribution as a product manager is enriching the company to grow its balance sheet. The product you are creating will lead to the company's growth from multiple aspects, such as creating new brands, goodwill (during mergers and acquisitions), trademarks and many other factors.

Secondly, the product's performance is considered by the control of cash-in and cash-out, i.e., the amount you are receiving from your customers for your product (accounts receivable) and the fees you are paying to your partners for providing the services (accounts payable).

We will touch upon three more elements of your balance sheet to discuss in detail. These are:

- **Prepaid Expenses**

    Prepaid expenses are the expenses related to the prepayment of services before they have occurred, i.e., the costs which are to happen at a future date, but the expenditure for the same is done. For example, premium payment of an insurance is a prepaid expense as the amount is spent in advance for the period, i.e., quarterly, half-yearly or annually.

- **Accounts Payable**

    Accounts payable are the current liabilities that have to be paid to your partners/vendors/suppliers for the services which have been taken on credit, without spending the cash up-front. For example, you might be engaging with multiple software service providers for the services needed for your application, wherein the service utilisation has started. Though, the payments are made later, depending on the terms & conditions negotiated during the agreement.

- **Accounts Receivable**

    Accounts receivable are the current assets on the balance sheet, wherein the word receivable refers to the payments that are yet to be accomplished. It means the services are comprehended, however, the money has still not hit the account. For example, an IT service provider, who is delivering services, will be expecting payments within a defined time frame as per the agreement. Therefore, the returns are an asset to the IT firm and are tagged under accounts receivable.

Income Statement

If, as a product owner, you are holding the P&L of the product, the income statement, which states its expenses, revenue and overall profit, will be very close to your heart. The income statement is generally known as the profit and loss statement, statement of income or statement of earnings.

Net income = Total revenue -Total expenses

Net income is also defined as net earnings or net profits.

ABC Corporation		
Income Statement		
For the period ending December 31, 2019		
Sales revenue		500,000
Cost of goods sold		100,000
	Gross profit	400,000
Operating expense		75,000
Depreciation expense		30,000
	EBIT	295,000
Interest expense		10,000
Income tax expense		8,000
	Net income	277,000

Key definitions around the income statement are:

- **Gross Profit**

    Gross profit is expressed as the difference between the total sales revenue and the cost of goods sold, i.e., the cost of goods or services sold to the customers. It does not include the operating cost and reflects how the business is performing by just considering the direct cost. For example, in the above case, the gross profit has been calculated as 400,000 USD (500,000 -100,000).

- **Gross Profit Margin**

    Gross profit margin, gross profit percentage or gross margin is calculated by gross profit divided by the sales revenue (net sales). In the above case, the gross profit percentage would be 80% (400,000 divided by 500,000).

- **Operating Earnings**

    Operating earnings, operating income or operating profit is calculated as gross profit minus total operating expenses. It ascertains the amount of money that has been generated by the company's operating activities. For example, in the above scenario, the operating income would be 295,000 USD (400,000 minus 75,000 minus 30,000). Interest expense and income tax expense are not considered as operating expenses, which gives rise to the term EBIT, expanded as 'Earnings Before Interest and Taxes', i.e., another name of Operating Income.

- **EBIDTA**

    EBIDTA is defined as earnings before interest, taxes, depreciation and amortization. It evaluates a company's operating performance.

    EBITDA = EBIT + Depreciation + Amortization

    There are two ways to calculate EBIDTA:

    - Take the operating income and add back the depreciation and amortization OR
    - Profit minus operating expense (excluding depreciation and amortization).

How to see an income statement from a product manager's point of view?

Budget allocation is one of the critical activities done in every organization. Multiple departments are asked to submit their budget proposals in terms of capital expenditure and operating expenditure. Product managers have this as one of their critical assignments, in which they share a forecast of the expected commercials that will come in place for the current financial year, for the products they are handling or any new product targeted for launch.

Aforementioned, it's crucial to understand where the P&L of the existing products' stand. Historical analysis of the statement will give you an indication of the cost, which has to be considered for the current year. Secondly, the budget sheet numbers should clearly articulate the requirements and should be backed by facts as to how it has been reported in the budget sheet (e.g., if a percentage increase is in consideration for the current year, it should articulate the reason).

Typically, the budget allocation should have goals which are planned to execute, backed with an income and expenses forecast. However, there can be potential events that can occur and may not have been initially accounted for. Therefore, keep a contingency budget in case of any unwanted expenses which can arise in the future. Otherwise, it might scale-down your existing budget.

Cash Flow Statement

The cash flow statement of a company reflects the inflow and outflow of cash and cash equivalents. For running the business, cash flows play a pivotal role as the business may go out of operation if enough liquidity is not maintained. Most companies fail due to poor management of cash flow.

Why does a small business fail?[1]

- 82% – Poor cash flow management skills or poor understanding of how the cash flow should be managed.

- 79% – Starting with too little money during the business set-up.

- 78% – Lack of a well-developed business plan, including insufficient research on the business before starting it.

- 77% – Not pricing properly or failure to include all necessary items when setting prices.

- 73% – Being overly optimistic about achievable sales, the money required and about what needs to be done to be successful.

- 70% – Not recognising or ignoring what they don't do well and not seeking help from those who do.

---

1   Hagen, Jessie. "of U.S. Bank cited on the SCORE/Counselors to America's Small Business website - www.score.org

The cash flow statement has three major categories, i.e., operating, investing and financing.

- **Operating Activities** – Cash from operating activities generated during regular business, within a specific period.

- **Investing Activities** – Cash from investing activities represents the purchase and sale of long-term investments.

- **Financing Activities** – Cash from financing activities represents long-term borrowing, short-term debt decrease, issuance and purchase of the company's bonds and stocks, payment of dividends to shareholders, etc.

ABC Corporation			
Cash Flow Statement			
For the period ending December 31, 2019			
Net income			277,000
Operating activities			
		Accounts receivable	(4,000)
		Inventories	(2,000)
		Prepaid expenses	(5,000)
		Accounts payable	4,000
		Income tax payable	8,000
		Wages payable	10,000
		Accrued expenses	17,000
		Total change in operating assets and liabilities	28,000
		Cash flow from operations	305,000
Investing activities			
		Sale of property, plant, and equipment	150,000
		Capital expenditure	(300,000)
		Cash flow from investing activities	(150,000)

Financing activities		
	Short term debt decrease	(2,000)
	Long term borrowing	30,000
	Capital stock	70,000
	Cash flow from investing activities	98,000
	Increase in cash during the year	253,000

Financial statement of a digital company (product based) – Is it worth justifying?

Oyo, a fast-growing hospitality business, reported a provisional net loss of 2384.69 crores INR for the financial year ending 2018-2019, which was up from the 360.43 crores INR of the previous fiscal year. Operating expenses jumped more than 390% to 6131.66 crores INR, while employee benefits and expenses rose nearly six-fold to 1538.85 crores INR. However, it still had a valuation of 5 billion USD for the financial year ending 2018-2019, and was getting more investments, though the income statement reflected in the negative, as expenses were much higher than the income. In November 2019, its valuation reached a whopping 10 billion USD.

Uber reported a loss of 1.8 billion USD in 2018, just before its IPO. In May 2019, when it went for a public offering, it valued the ride-hailing company at 82.4 billion USD. In 2016, Microsoft acquired LinkedIn at 26.2 billion USD. However, just four months before the acquisition, LinkedIn's share price plunged 44% in one day, when they announced a bad quarter and lowered forecasts. Facebook acquired WhatsApp for 19 billion USD in 2014, when WhatsApp had no revenues or profits.

In 2018, an article originally published under the English title "**Why Financial Statements Don't Work for Digital Companies**[2]", highlights

---

2   From "Why Financial Statements Don't Work for Digital Companies" by Vijay Govindarajan, Shivaram Rajagopal, and Anup Srivastava, February 6, 2018. Copyright © 2020 Harvard Business School Publishing. All rights reserved.

why investors react negatively to financial statement losses for an industrial firm but disregard such losses for a digital firm.

There is an interesting fact discussed on tangible and intangible investments. In the case of a manufacturing firm, there is a clear indication of the inventories, assets, land building, machinery and other equipment types. However, in the case of a digital firm, most of the assets are intangible, i.e., Trademark, Goodwill, Patents, Brand Name and Software.

The building block of digital companies include elements such as:

- Organizational Strategy
- Research and Development
- Software and Data
- Peer and Supplier Networks
- Human Capital
- Products
- Brands

Many digital companies have no physical assets and no inventory to report. Investments by digital companies are more into the building blocks as mentioned above, and are not capitalised as assets. They are treated as expenses during the calculation of income. Hence, during the initial growth stage of a digital company, it reports higher losses in its income statement. Investors must disregard their earnings in investment decisions.

From "Why We Need to Update Financial Reporting for the Digital Era" by Vijay Govindarajan, Shivaram Rajagopal, and Anup Srivastava, June 8, 2018. Copyright © 2020 Harvard Business School Publishing. All rights reserved.

From "A Blueprint for Digital Companies' Financial Reporting" by Vijay Govindarajan, Shivaram Rajagopal, and Anup Srivastava, August 3, 2018. Copyright © 2020 Harvard Business School Publishing. All rights reserved.

Also, in the case of digital companies, the value of their intangible assets, brand value and user base increases, contradictory to the manufacturing companies (machinery), wherein the value of the asset depreciates.

Therefore, the balance sheet of a physical and digital company gives a different picture.

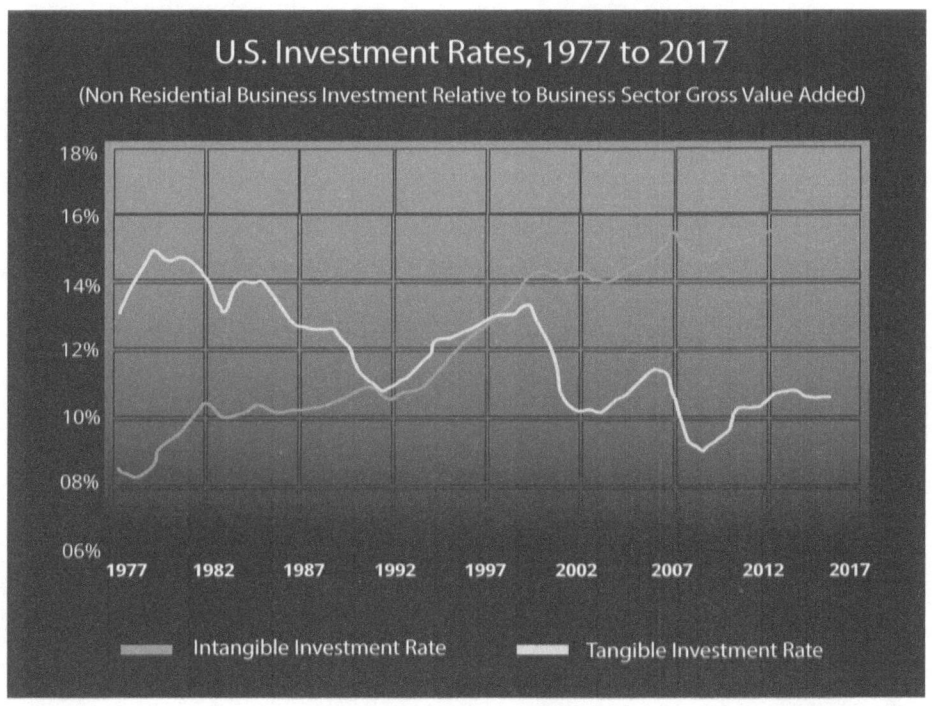

Source – InstaInvest

"The End of Accounting and the Path Forward for Investors and Managers", authored by Baruch Lev and Feng Gu, mentions in their book that "The remedy for corporate earnings problem lies in the systematic disclosure of information that focuses on the fundamentals of the business, such as customer acquisition costs, additions and churn rate for internet, telecom and media companies; the progress and risk diversification of the product pipeline of pharma and biotech firms; capacity utilization and route changes (coverage) of transportation enterprises; or frequency and severity of claims for insurance companies."

These are forward-looking indicators for performance and growth, highlighting the strategy of the business and the success of its execution. Certain companies provide such information in conference calls or management discussion and analysis, but this is done haphazardly and inconsistently. Some companies do not offer it at all, making it impossible to analyse and compare companies systematically.

As a product manager, your focus should be on building such a product which provides value addition to the targeted customers and is backed by the research w.r.t. customer needs. Get your trademark, wordmark and domain registered, and file for the patent if you are creating an exclusive proposition with the latest technology. All these will add to the growth of intangible assets and will bring in more investment to the firm.

Privacy Really Matters

I have shared my personal information with the company, including my personal data such as my name, email ID and contact details. However, I do not want to keep any personal information with them as I haven't availed of any service. Also, I want them to delete my information and convey that my request has been completed because, for me, privacy truly matters.

An organization needs to keep the information safe and protect their customers, employees and partners, providing them with the data, whenever they need, as to what kind of information has been captured by the institution. Personal data has real value, therefore, organizations have a legal duty to ensure that the data is safe and secured.

Some of the recent fines by the **Information Commissioner's Office** (ICO), which have been imposed, will give you a shudder as to how it may setback the entire business.

ICO Announcement of $124 million fine for Marriott International on July 9, 2019, following the data breach.

ICO issued a notice of its intention to fine Marriott International a sum of £99,200,396 (approx. 124 Million USD), for infringements of the General Data Protection Regulation (GDPR). The proposed fine was related to a cyber incident that was notified to the ICO by Marriott, in November 2018. A variety of personal data, of approximately 339 million guest records globally, was exposed by the incident, of which around 30 million was related to residents of 31 countries in the European Economic Area (EEA), whereas seven million was associated with UK residents.

It is conceded that the vulnerability began when the systems of the Starwood Hotel Group were compromised in 2014. Marriott subsequently acquired Starwood in 2016, but the exposure of customer information was not discovered until 2018. The ICO's investigation found that Marriott failed to undertake sufficient due diligence when it bought Starwood, and should also have done more to secure its systems.

ICO Intention to fine British Airways £183.39M under GDPR for the data breach on July 8, 2019.

ICO issued a notice of its intention to fine British Airways a sum of £183.39M for infringements of the General Data Protection Regulation (GDPR). The proposed fine relates to a cyber incident notified to the ICO by British Airways, in September 2018. In part, this incident involved user traffic to the British Airways website being diverted to a fraudulent site. Through this malicious website, attackers harvested the customer details. Personal data of approximately 500,000 customers was compromised in this incident, which is believed to have begun in June 2018.

The ICO's investigation found that a variety of information was jeopardised by inadequate security arrangements at the company, including login, payment card, travel booking details as well as name and address information.

International airline fined £500,000 for failing to secure its customers' personal data on 4th March, 2020.

The Information Commissioner's Office (ICO) fined Cathay Pacific Airways Limited a sum of £500,000 for inadequacy to protect its customers' personal data security. The airline's failure to secure its systems, resulted in unauthorised access to their passengers' private details, including names, passport and identity details, dates of birth, postal and email addresses, phone numbers and historical travel information.

Cathay Pacific became aware of suspicious activity in March 2018, when its database was subjected to a brute force attack, where numerous passwords or phrases are submitted with the hope of eventually guessing correctly.

The incident led Cathay Pacific to employ a cyber security firm, and they subsequently reported the incident to the ICO.

From an organization standpoint, two important activities need to be wholly recognised and implemented i.e., Data Protection and Data Privacy. Data protection means keeping the data safe from unauthorised access while Data privacy means empowering control to the users to make their own decisions as to who can process their data and for what purposes.

Personal Data

Personal data is any information which correlates to an identified or identifiable natural person, whether directly or indirectly. It includes information such as name, address, date of birth, account numbers and other identifiers such as usernames, IP addresses, location and mobile device IDs. Personal data that is encrypted, de-identified or pseudonymised, but can be used to re-identify a person, remains personal data and falls within reach of the GDPR. Personal data that is anonymous, so that the individual is no longer identifiable, is no longer considered personal data.

Sensitive Personal Data – Personal data that consists of lifestyle identifiers (religion, sexual orientation, etc.), health and finances, political information, genetic data and biometric data are all considered to be sensitive personal data.

Personal Data	Sensitive Personal Data
• Names	• Racial or ethnic origin
• Addresses	• Political opinions
• Dates of birth	• Religious or philosophical beliefs
• Credit card numbers	• Trade union membership
• Government ID numbers	• Health or sex life
• E-mail addresses	• Genetic data
• Account numbers	• Biometric data
• Location data	
• Pseudonymous data	

All the above personal data-related information belongs to a person, who is called a **"Data Subject"**.

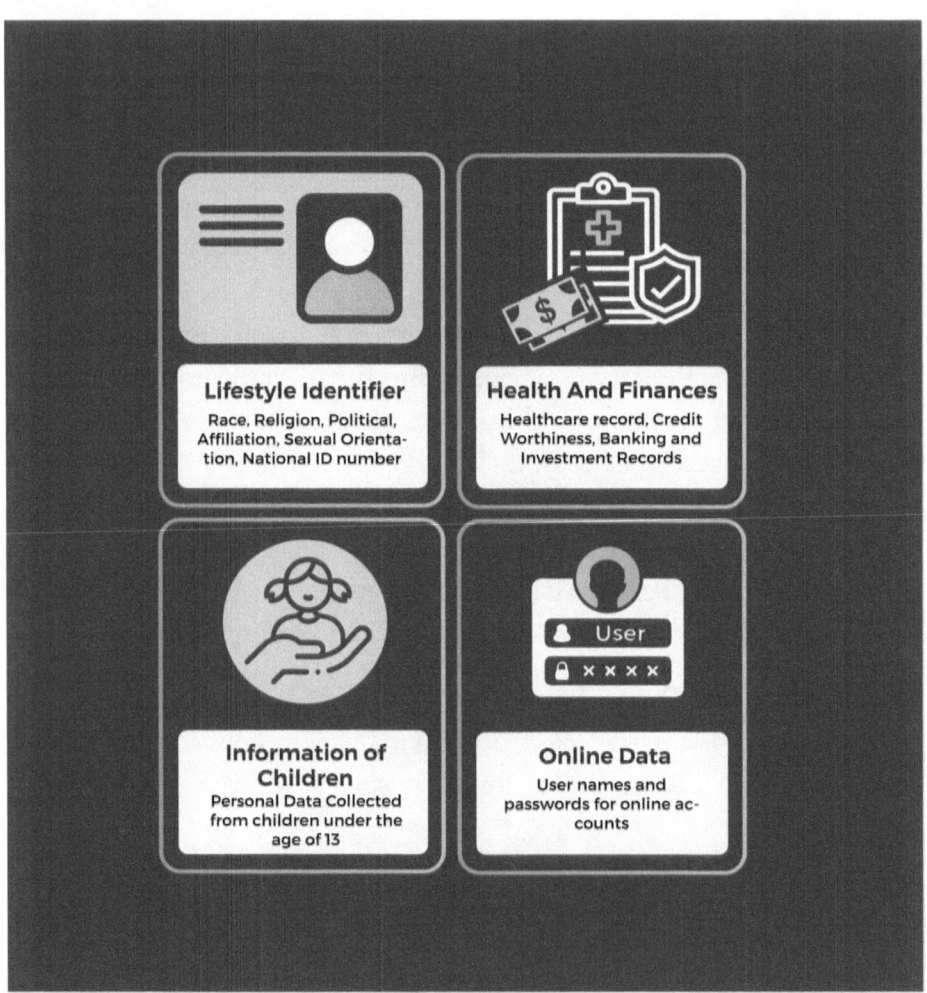

Global Privacy Laws

Requirements concerning privacy vary from country to country. It is not required to be an expert on each country's privacy laws to protect your organization. However, it is vital to be aware and abide by the regulations in the countries or regions where the business is continuing.

Note: As a product manager, it is of utmost importance to understand the type of information sent to your partner and how they are processing it.

Therefore, it is critically important to assess your partner and complete the Data Protection Impact Assessment (DPIA).

DPIA

DPIA requirement is for every partner with whom you are onboarding for your product requirement, wherein the partner is involved in processing the customer's personal information. It is a process that assists in systematically analysing, identifying and minimising the data protection risks of a project or product. It is a vital part of the accountability obligations under the GDPR, and when done accurately, it helps you assess and demonstrate how to comply with all the data protection obligations.

Conducting a DPIA is a legal requirement for any processing, including certain specified types of processing that are likely to result in a high risk to individuals' rights and freedom. Under GDPR, failure to carry out a DPIA, when required, may leave you open to enforcement action, including a fine of up to €10 million or a 2% of the global annual turnover, if higher.

Note: General Data Protection Regulation (GDPR) strengthens and unifies protection for EU citizens' personal data and clearly defines the limits for the transfer and processing of such data outside the EU.

Let's say you are onboarding a partner, who is providing you with payment gateway services. You should know all the aspects of the DPIA so that you can evaluate the vendor and identify the associated risks. For example:

- What type of personal data is being stored by your partner?
- Do they have any sub-processors?
- Where and who hosts the data for them?
- Do they have an internal security/privacy policy in place?
- How is sensitive personal data being stored? What are the encryption mechanisms?
- For what purpose is the partner collecting the data? Is it legitimate to provide the services?

For all product managers out there - I know this is boring to fill in. However, don't consider it as one of the activities to just do. It has a more significant impact and might cause legal actions as well. Therefore, it's of utmost importance to implement the outcomes from the assessment of your DPIA into your project plan and continue it on an ongoing basis, if there are any further changes and involves reassessment.

Reference to Sample DPIA document - https://ico.org.uk/media/for-organisations/documents/2553993/dpia-template.docx

Data Controller Vs Data Processor

Every organization that handles data must safeguard it, but according to the GDPR, an organization's specific responsibility depends on whether it is a Data Processor or a Data Controller.

A Data Controller collects the data. It determines the purpose for which and the means by which the data will be processed. Collected data can be used for their own processes or shared with an external service provider to work with and provide service to customers. The data controller will always remain in control by specifying how the data will be used and processed by the external service provider.

A Data Processor processes the data on behalf of the data controller. The data processor is usually a third party, external to the company. These third parties, neither own the data nor do they control it. They will not be able to change the purpose and means for which the data is used. Furthermore, data processors are bound by the instructions given by the data controller.

For example, if you are using the Google tag manager on your company's website to track the number of visitors, most popular pages, time spent, etc., then all this information will be captured in Google Analytics via the Google tag manager. Your company needs to share this data with Google to get the insights they want from Google Analytics. Here, the data controller is the company on whose website the customer is visiting, and the data processor is Google Tag/Google Analytics.

Privacy Principles of GDPR

1. **Lawfulness, Fairness and Transparency** – There are several lawful bases for processing information, i.e., Consent, Contract, Legal Obligation, Vital Interests, Public Task and Legitimate Interest. Fairness, as the name suggests, specifies how you collect your data and how you use it. Transparency requires to have a privacy policy that outlines several activities in clear terms, but is not limited to the following - What data you collect; Why you need the data and how you are processing it; Whether you share with third parties, etc.

2. **Limitations on Purposes of Collection, Processing and Storage** – Information to be collected for specified, explicit and legitimate purposes, and should not be processed further in a manner that is incompatible with those purposes.

3. **Data Minimisation** – Refers to adequate, relevant and limited data collection to only what is necessary to the purposes for which it is being processed.

4. **Accuracy of Data** - Accurate and, where necessary, kept up to date. Every reasonable step is taken into consideration to ensure that personal data that is inaccurate, regarding the purposes for which they are processed, is erased or rectified without delay.

5. **Data Storage Limits** - Kept in a form which permits identification of data subjects for no longer than is necessary (retention schedule), for the purposes for which personal data is processed.

6. **Integrity and Confidentiality** - Processed in a manner that ensures appropriate security of the personal data, including protection against unauthorised or unlawful processing as well as against accidental loss, destruction or damage, using appropriate technical or organizational measures.

The data controller shall be accountable and responsible to display compliance with the earlier mentioned six principles ('accountability').

As mentioned above, the requirement of data privacy laws varies from country to country. Hence, Canada also has its own ten principles of Personal Information Protection and Electronic Documents Act (PIPEDA). These principles are named as:

1. Accountability
2. Identifying Purposes
3. Consent
4. Limiting Collection
5. Limiting Use, Disclosure and Retention
6. Accuracy
7. Safeguards
8. Openness
9. Individual Access
10. Challenging Compliance

Rights of Individuals

The rights of individuals or data subjects (customers of our product) are about their rights related to the information shared with the company. Below are the rights which an individual possesses.

- **Right to be informed** - To provide the data subject with the ability to ask a company for information regarding the type of personal data being processed and the rationale for processing it.

- **Right of access to personal data** – Providing the data subject with the ability to get access to the personal data that is being processed.

- **Right to rectification** - Providing the data subject with the ability to ask for modifications to their personal data, in case the data subject believes that the data is not up-to-date or accurate.

- **Right to erasure** - Providing the data subject with the ability to ask for deletion of the data.

- **Right to data portability** – Providing the data subject the ability to ask for the personal data to be provided back or shifted to another controller.

- **Right to object** – Providing the data subject with the ability to object to the processing of their personal data.

- **Right to restriction of processing** - Providing the data subject the right to restrict the processing of personal data for limited purposes only.

- **Rights regarding automated decision making** – Providing the ability to object to a decision based on automated processing. In accordance with this right, a customer may ask for his or her request to be reviewed manually.

As a product manager, when you are developing the product or when you are in the initial stages of the process flow creation, do ensure the elements that will come in place for user privacy are accounted for. The user will have all the fundamental rights apropos data that is shared. It is essential to have "**Privacy by Design**" while developing the product, with privacy as a priority along with other purposes the product serves.

There are seven foundation principles of privacy by design, which are explained below.

1. **Proactive not Reactive; Preventative not Remedial** – It anticipates and prevents privacy-invasive events before they occur. Privacy and security should be an indispensable part of the product from the beginning.

2. **Privacy as Default Setting** - Privacy should be there by default and the personal data should be protected automatically, in any given IT system. If an individual does nothing, their privacy should remain intact.

3. **Privacy Embedded into Design** – Privacy to be embedded into the design and architecture of IT systems and business practices. Privacy must be integrated into operations, technologies and architectures in a holistic, integrative and creative way.

4. **Full Functionality — Positive-Sum, not Zero-Sum** – Accommodating all legitimate interests and objectives in a positive-sum and not through a zero-sum approach, where unnecessary trade-offs are performed. It also avoids the pretence of false dichotomies, such as privacy vs. security, demonstrating that it is possible and far more desirable to have both.

5. **End-to-End Security – Full Lifecycle Protection** – Strong security measures should be taken from start to finish. It ensures all the data is securely maintained and then securely destroyed at the end of the process, on time.

6. **Visibility and Transparency – Keep it Open** – Visibility and transparency are essential to establish accountability and trust, thus, allowing users and other stakeholders to see how information flows from one system to another.

7. **Respect for User Privacy – Keep it User-Centric** - Keep the interests of the individual topmost by offering measures such as robust privacy defaults, appropriate notices and empowering user-friendly options. Keep it user-centric!

Thinking Strategically

Strategic thinking plays a crucial role in the organization. It is looking at things from a macro perspective rather than keeping your work or ideas confined. Start looking at information from a broader perspective and you will start getting noticed in the organization. The management would like to elevate your career and begin functioning with them.

Apart from your workstream, you should know the different products and services that the organization serves to its customers. It will assist you in thinking at a more strategic level about what kind of new products and services can be pioneered for the company.

However, thinking strategically is not that easy unless you are highly motivated and possess certain qualities, from being agile to balancing your consistency.

Defining Strategy

Strategy is defined as a broader view of the objective or the task accomplished with a plan or method, thus, achieving a desired future state. It is inferred from the Greek word "strategos", which means "general".

According to Henry Mintzberg, the author of "The Rise and Fall of Strategic Planning", strategy can be defined in multiple ways.

- It is a plan, a means of getting from here to there, i.e., a 'how'.
- It is a model in actions over time.

- It is a position, that is, it reflects decisions to offer products or services markets.
- It is perspective, that is, vision and direction.

According to Michael Porter (1996), Competitive Strategy is "**about being different**". He detailed that strategy is about competitive positioning, differentiating yourself in the eyes of the customer and adding value through a mix of activities, different from those used by competitors.

According to Benjamin Tregoe and John Zimmerman (1980), Business Strategy is a framework that supervises the choices, which determine the nature and direction of an organization. Ultimately, this boils down to selecting products (or services) to offer and the markets in which to offer them. Though, there are nine possible driving forces, however, only one can serve as the basis for a strategy for a given business. The nine driving forces are listed below.

- Products offered
- Production capability
- Natural resources
- Market needs
- Method of sale
- Size/growth
- Technology
- Method of distribution
- Return/profit

According to Michael Robert, in his book "**Strategy Pure & Simple**", he has spoken about the four main factors that drive strategy:

- Products & Services
- Customers

- Market Segments
- Geographic Areas

These are further compelled by external driving forces and only one can be the basis for strategy. The ten driving forces cited are:

- Product-service
- Sales-marketing method
- User-customer
- Distribution method
- Market type
- Natural resources
- Production capacity-capability
- Size/growth
- Technology
- Return/profit

Strategy Hierarchies

Strategy of an organization begins from its vision statement, as to what is the desired status it wants to achieve. It has either an overarching strategy or a corporate strategy, which is derived from the vision statement that includes the goals, priorities and focus that needs to be pursued over a period.

From an individual standpoint, to follow a particular path, it is essential to take guidance as to which route needs to be considered. If you don't follow the right direction, you might take an inappropriate path, which further results in a waste of time and effort. Similarly, from an organization standpoint, Vision, Mission and Value statements play a critical role in guiding the individuals to follow the right path for the organization's growth story.

It is imperative for product managers to align the product's goal with the organization's Vision and Mission, keeping the code of ethics, i.e., Values, in consideration. If you are developing a new product, set its vision and mission statement, and start working in the right direction from the very beginning. This will always give you a complete sense of direction. Though, some elements of your new product's vision are changed in the current agile world, I would recommend a quick adaptation without impacting the overall product goal. Remember not to go for frequent changes in the vision statement of your new product development, as it might negatively affect your stakeholders (why the product strategy is changing so frequently?).

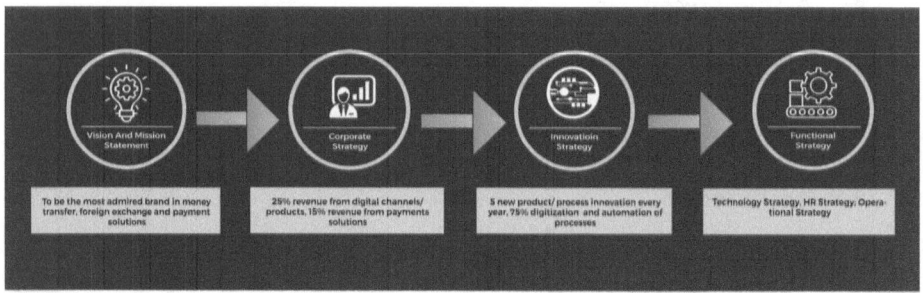

Vision Statement

Vision statement refers to the organization's overarching aspiration, i.e., the future state which it desires to achieve or become. It is a broader perspective of the organization, which should be concise and very clearly defined.

Example: UAE Exchange

"To be the most admired brand in Money Transfer, Foreign Exchange and Payment Solutions"

Example: Flipkart

"To become Amazon of India"

Mission Statement

What the organization will do to get there to achieve their vision, is called a mission statement. Most of the organizations don't specify it or use the term vision and mission, interchangeably. However, having a defined mission is a step towards defining strategic goals, which signify the key objectives and is more actionable.

Example: Flipkart

"Ab har wish hogi puri" i.e. Now every wish will get fulfilled

Values

Value statements are primarily the code of ethics or the core values that organizations need to adopt to achieve their vision and mission. It represents what the organization believes in and how employees are expected to communicate with each other, with customers, stakeholders and external partners.

Example: UAE Exchange

"Our core values – Integrity, Commitment, Empowerment and Care"

Example: Flipkart

"Core values - Customer First, Ownership, Bias For Action, Audacity and Respect"

Corporate and Business Strategy

Corporate strategy is a multifaceted organizational strategy, where the focus is on everything from launching of products to entering into new markets, understanding competitors, and positioning the business uniquely, where it wants to operate and compete. In short, it is defined as the "**company's portfolio**" and reflects the company's long term strategy towards growth and prospects.

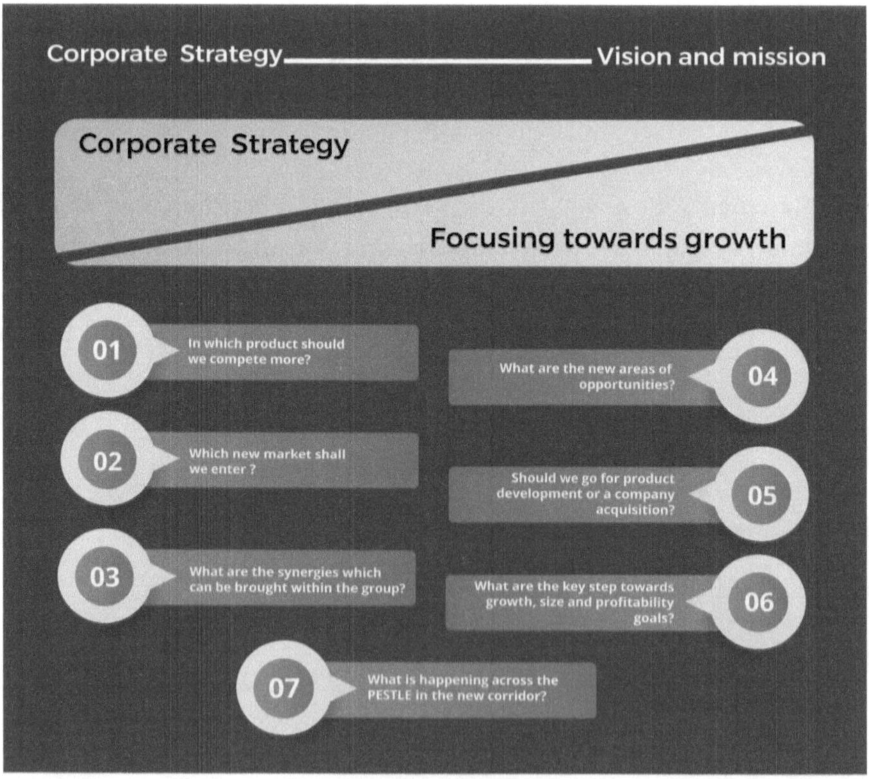

![Corporate Strategy diagram: Corporate Strategy — Vision and mission; Focusing towards growth. 01 In which product should we compete more? 02 Which new market shall we enter? 03 What are the synergies which can be brought within the group? 04 What are the new areas of opportunities? 05 Should we go for product development or a company acquisition? 06 What are the key step towards growth, size and profitability goals? 07 What is happening across the PESTLE in the new corridor?]

Innovation Strategy

Innovation plays a critical role in the organization's success, and hence, should be given utmost importance. There should always be a specific department where people of the company, who are inclined towards long term objectives, think strategically and love building products, should work. It's vital to have the right set of people in innovation as it is not everyone's cup of tea. A person needs to be agile, have curiosity and balance the consistency as well.

I remember my tenure in ICICI Bank, which always gave high priority to digital innovation. That is why it is referred to as the most tech-savvy bank in India. People see the bank as a "first-of-a-kind" service provider, because it has always been a prospector for new initiatives, and whatever it does, the market adopts as an analyser. We will study more about analyser and prospector strategy in the latter part of this section.

Innovation strategy focuses not only on new product development but also on existing process improvement and service innovation. New digital business models are generated by innovation/discovery, which adds as an asset to the organization. However, many people in the organization might be averse to innovation. They might say – "Why is the organization spending so much on this new product?", "We are already running a similar kind of business", "Why has this been approved?", "I don't see any value add to it", "It's a wastage of money, time and effort, rather the company should have paid bonuses to us."

Remember, different people have different views. However, the management looks at innovation in different scales and understands its importance. They know where they need to pump the money to cater to the gen-next products as well as the importance of the past, present and future, and manage all three together. That is why they are called visionaries, as they can analyse the future with a broader mindset and are open to change.

There are several examples in the industry of companies who didn't innovate and thought that their ongoing business model was perfect and that they were catering to a large section of the society at present. However, they don't exist now since they never focused on disruptive innovation.

Kodak Moments

A Kodak moment, gone forever, has left long-lasting memories. Every millennial can correlate to it, as most of them were kodak fans or I would say, everyone was a Kodak fan, because nothing was digitised at that point in time, and people carried Kodak reels to get them printed.

Many evangelists pointed out that Kodak's inability to see digital photography as a disruptive technology continued to remain for decades, despite their research team also pointing to this. The research efforts led by the internal team had mentioned about the core technologies and the likely adoption curve. They positioned both, the pros and cons, mentioning that digital photography could replace Kodak's established business, but it might take some time to occur. Even though Kodak had a longer window of opportunity, they couldn't materialise on it with the right strategic choices.

Steve Sasson, an engineer in Kodak, who was the inventor of the digital camera, led to the contribution of the patent licensing's success. Despite this, by the 1980s, digital cameras were squeezing the profit margins from Kodak in the consumer space. However, the high-profit margin in photo film sales, i.e., around 70-80%, and consumer electronics business, which had 3-4%, was never a focused transition area for CEO Whitmore. Mr. Whitmore said he would make sure Kodak stayed closer to its core businesses in film and photographic chemicals.

George Fisher, who was the successor to Whitmore, mentioned that Kodak related digital photography as the enemy, an evil juggernaut that would kill the chemical-based film and paper business that had fuelled Kodak's sales and profits for decades. In 2005, Kodak brought in CEO Antonio Perez, who came from HP, and saw the future in consumer printers. He, however couldn't change the culture of Kodak and faced difficulty in dealing with the legacy of Kodak's leadership. On January 19th, 2012, Eastman Kodak filed for bankruptcy.

Note: Eastman Kodak lost the appeal of the patent dispute over digital image preview technology with Apple Inc and Research In Motion Ltd., which set back the photography giant's efforts to raise money in bankruptcy by selling patents.

Innovation Strategy Frameworks

Porter's generic strategic framework

Michael Porter, in his book "Competitive Advantage: Creating and Sustaining Superior Performance", identified strategies to achieve a competitive edge. These strategies are Cost Leadership, Differentiation and Focus Strategy. He further divided the focus strategy into cost focus and differentiation focus.

Let's understand them in detail so that we know which strategy to apply under what circumstances.

Cost Leadership: Minimising the organization's cost for delivery of products and services, i.e., reducing the operating cost to increase profits. If your operating cost is less, you can increase the market share by offering the product at a competitive price to the customers or have a larger market share with average prices. It will create an edge and bring in more customers who are cost-conscious.

Example: Cross border remittance market is immensely competitive. Therefore, to get more customers initially, the company might squeeze its profit and position themselves as the instant money transfer company without any additional charge from customers, by providing the best-assured rate (competitive forex margin).

There are both pros and cons to this strategy. As a product manager, you should always know for which product/feature this should be used.

Pros:

- Company can improve its market share by offering the product at a lower cost.
- Get more marketing visibility by positioning as the low-cost service provider.
- Brings more efficiency by optimising several processes.

Cons:

- It will directly hit the P&L and squeeze the profit of the company.
- Customer can also go to another competitor if the quality decreases with the price.
- Other competitors can also reduce their cost, and there will be a further challenging task to manage both price reduction and profit.
- Company must have substantial capital at their disposal.

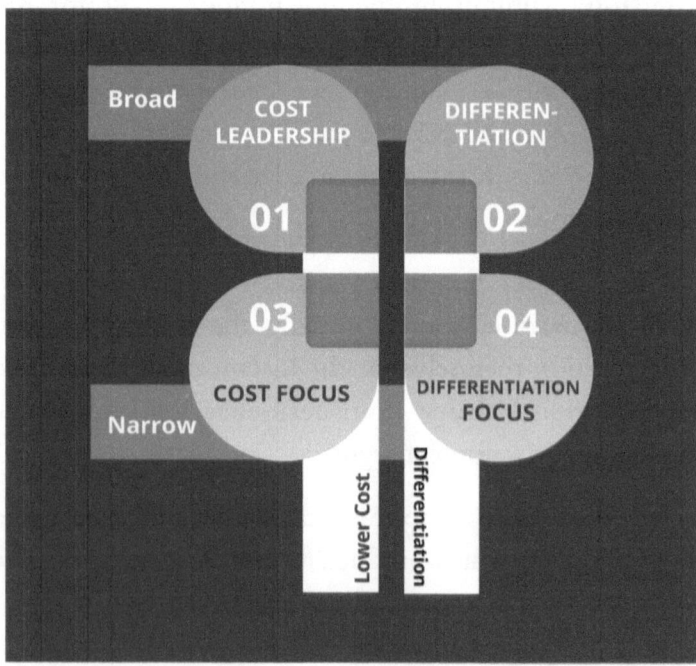

Differentiation Strategy: Creating differentiation in your product by delivering unique, attractive or high-quality products, features and services as compared to your competitors, by building a high-value brand image, providing excellent services to your customers, driving innovation and creativity, thus, bringing in all the differentiation. As most of these brands focus on the new trends in the industry, therefore, customers start looking at such brands as industry differentiators and always desire constant innovation from them.

Pros:

- Build a powerful digital brand image among the customers.
- Drive the culture of research & development and innovation within the organization.
- Organization becomes more flexible and is always ready to adapt to change (else it might go like Kodak).
- Companies can have better margins in specific products as differentiation has already been provided.

Cons:

- Agility is important to be maintained throughout or the competitors might come with a new differentiation.
- Launching products/features without a value proposition can lead to a significant reduction in the market share.

Focus Strategy: Focus strategy concentrates on the products and services for a niche market (narrow market focus), by understanding the market's dynamics and what the customer needs unique within that market. Is the customer looking for a low-cost product or a product with a unique or innovative set of features?

- In the case of Cost Focus Strategy – the company targets the niche market to ensure the focus remains towards offering at the lowest possible price.

- In the case of Differentiation Focus - the company targets the niche market to ensure the focus remains towards offering unique/innovative product and features.

Pros:

- Good control of the niche market.
- Opportunity to generate high margins.
- A better understanding of customers and providing solutions accordingly.

Cons:

- Too much dependency on single markets comes with a huge risk and will take the focus out from the broad markets.
- Introduction of new technologies can lead to the product being outdated.

Pisano Innovation Landscape Map

Every company has its strategic model, however, when it comes to innovation, they need to think from a broader perspective and analyse where they must allocate their funds to achieve growth. Is it technology advancement or a strong business model?

Let us understand the matrix presented by Pisano, which describes how potential innovation fits within the company.

Thinking Strategically | **45**

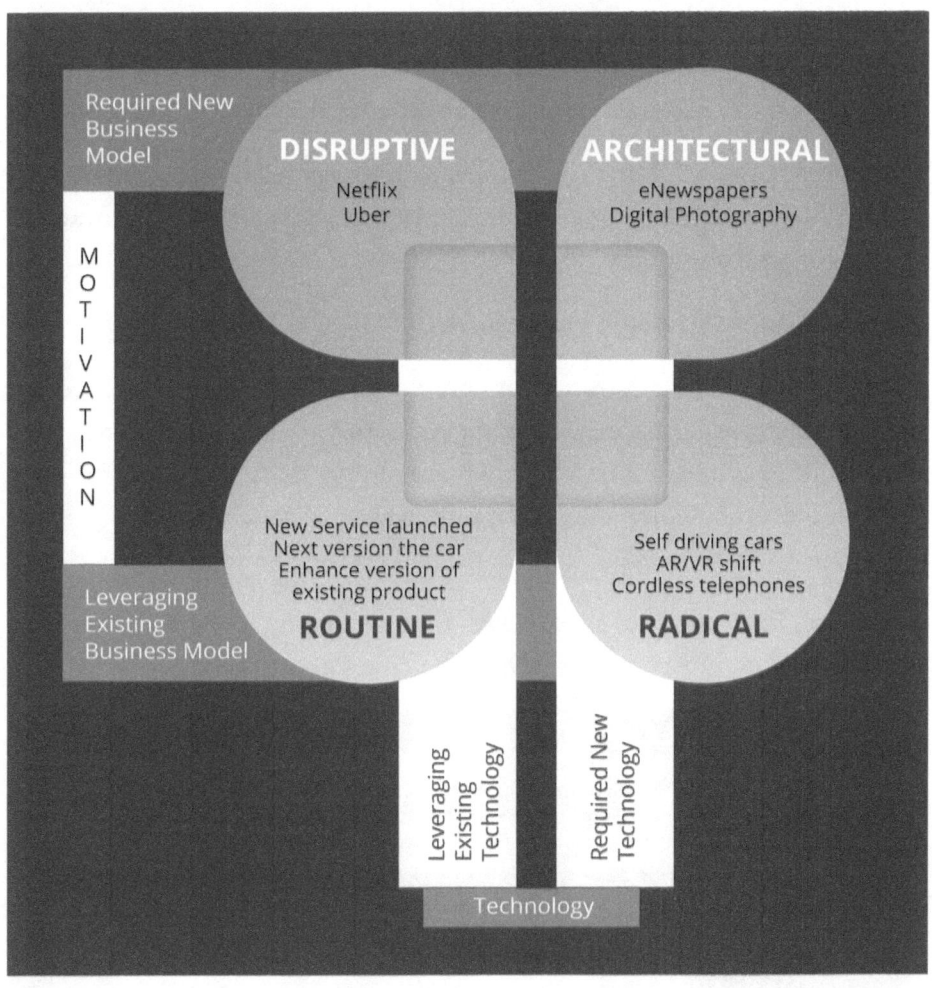

From "You need an Innovation Strategy" by Gary P. Pisano, June 2018. Copyright © 2020 Harvard Business School Publishing. All rights reserved.

Disruptive Innovation: It focuses on a new business model but not necessarily cutting-edge technology. It is also referred to as Stealth Innovation.

Architectural Innovation: As the name suggests, it is an architectural change, i.e., combined focus on both business and technology.

Routine Innovation: It focuses on leveraging the existing technology competency that the company has, and driving the existing business models with a new set of features, leading to an enhanced version of the model.

Radical Innovation: It focuses on new technology relative to what already exists. When we think more about innovation, it's about radical innovation, i.e., creating revolutionary technology.

Miles and Snow Strategic Framework

Miles and Snow's strategy framework provides businesses an approach to the right set of strategies in order to compete in the market. Many companies want to innovate, which is why they are always the first-to-market ones while some other companies adopt to wait-and-watch, analysing what others are doing to manage innovation and cost.

There are four specific approaches that are being considered in this framework, i.e., Prospector, Analyser, Defender and Reactor.

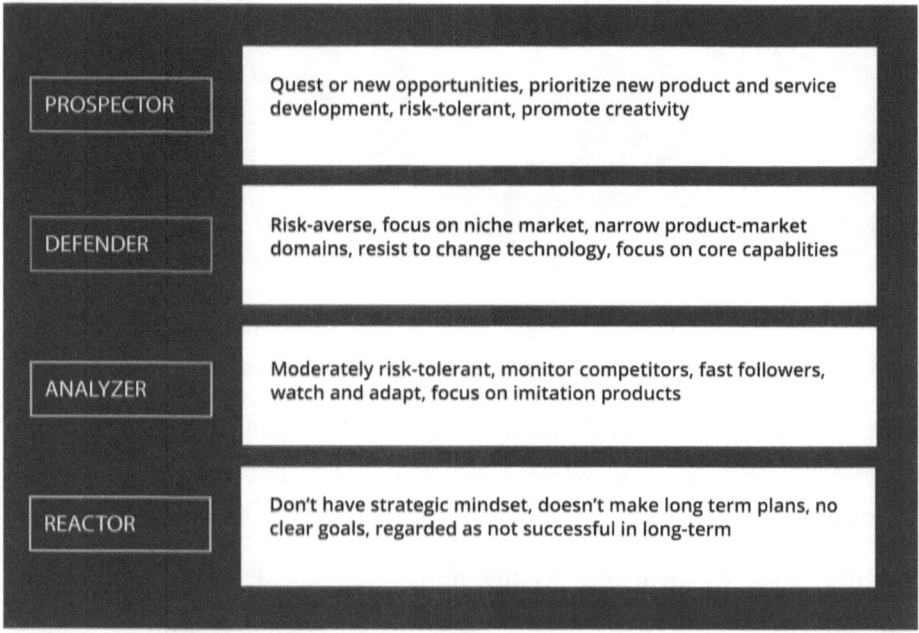

Companies adopt different strategies depending on the business environment and the market in which they operate. No single strategic

orientation is the best. Each plan can position a company differently in the market so that they can respond and adapt (expect reactor).

Survey – Is it a Vision or a Customer?

A survey was conducted on LinkedIn to seek the customer's input w.r.t. new product development. The survey was based on the questionnaire - **When you go for a new product development, which is the most critical driving factor you consider for the new idea?** The result is depicted in the graph below.

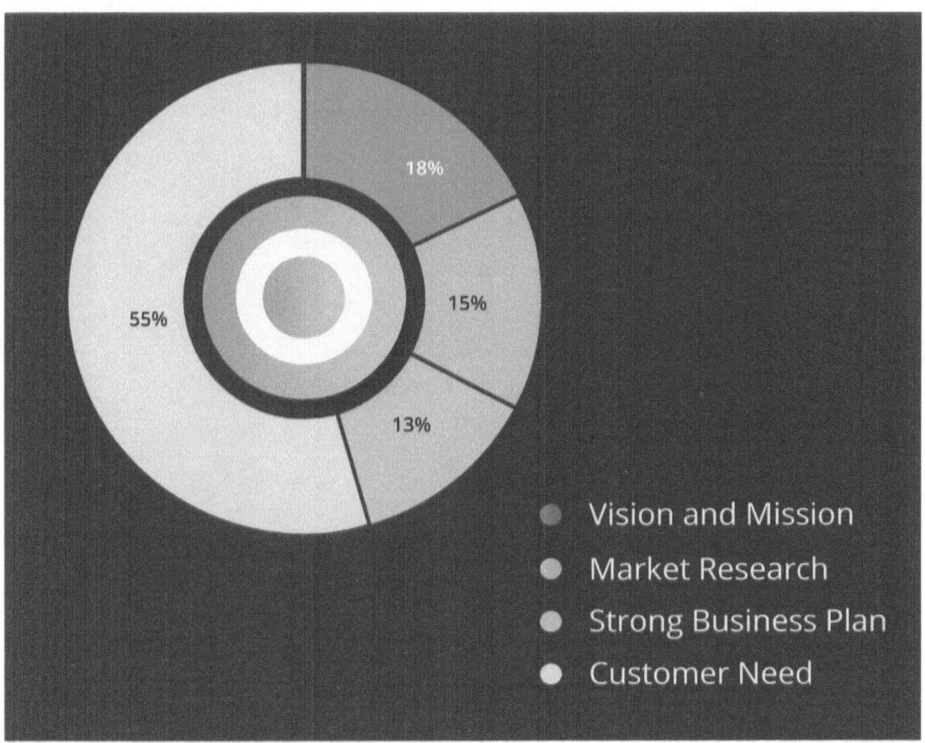

The graph, unquestionably portrays the customer as a winner, but there were interesting numbers around other parameters as well, which I thought might be quite less. The organization's vision and mission stood at 18% and was the second driving factor after the customer's need.

One of the customers wrote – "My viewpoint is that customers never had a requirement for an iPod, and no market research companies stressed the importance of it. However, the vision and mission lead to a strong business plan."

Another customer wrote – "I too believe that mission and vision are the driving factors for product development, but having said this, I feel that without a strong business model, any product will fail. Having an idea for a product is great, but without a plan to monetise, the product will result in a loss. Facebook, when it started, had a strong vision to connect with people, but they also had a strong business plan to generate revenue through advertisements. Hence, my view is that vision and strong business plans, both are quintessential for developing a new product."

Building the Right Product

I have an idea and I want to propose a new product to the organization for its long-term strategy. However, whether the idea generated is worth or not? How can a concept's credibility be checked? There are several ways to create the idea innovatively. It is truly mentioned that innovation doesn't come naturally, it comes with practice. Hence, you need to practice it.

Let us understand the first step towards generating new ideas or new features and whether actual users need such kind of products. This process is called "**Product Discovery**".

Product Discovery

As the name itself suggests, it is about discovering products. Let's find out whether our users or customers are really in need of such products. Product discovery tends to reduce indecision and assist in eliminating any second thoughts on whether to proceed with the product preliminaries. Everything in product discovery starts from having a profound understanding of your customer base.

David Kelly, Founder of IDEO & the Stanford d.school, coined "Design Thinking" as a human-centred path to innovation. He mentioned that everybody is creative, and knowing the right approach to design thinking can lead to innovative, creative and astonishing ideas. Create something which makes the customer's life better, is also feasible to produce and makes business sense.

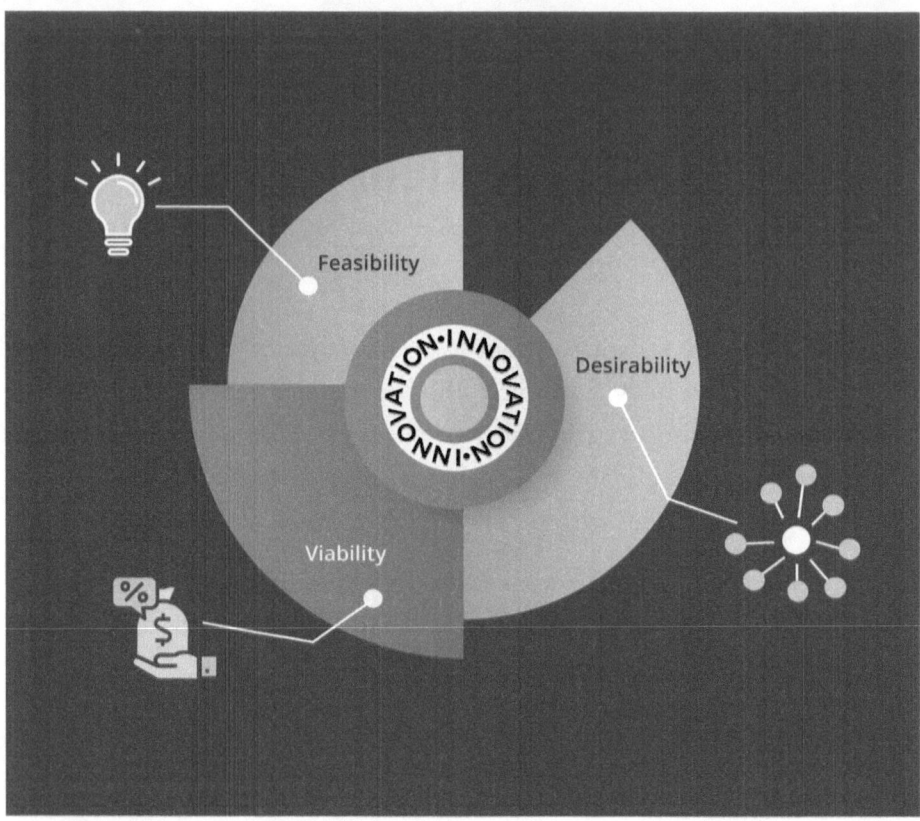

The above diagram depicts where innovation is positioned, centred at the heart of feasibility, viability and desirability.

- **Feasibility:** Is the idea that has been thought feasible or not? Is it targeted for the current customer segment or focused on next-gen customers?

- **Viability:** Does the idea make business sense? Will it generate revenue or drive-in more customers? Is it viable to spend money on this?

- **Desirability:** Will the customer like this idea? What is their desire for this? Do they seem to be interested or do we need to generate an interest for this product?

Let us understand the process of design thinking, which should be accomplished during the product discovery phase.

Double Diamond Approach

As mentioned above, while discussing the desirability of the idea/product, it is important to understand your customers, the issues they are facing and how you can resolve those with new ways of creative and intuitive ideas.

The double diamond approach provides a comprehensive way to understand your customers. It consists of two types of thinking, i.e., Divergent and Convergent.

- **Divergent Thinking** – Think as much as you can, don't restrict your thinking. Think from a macro perspective, go deep as much as you can.

- **Convergent Thinking** – Think on a micro level, start focusing on a few problems and their solutions arrived from divergent thinking. Bring your observations back and start paying attention to the real customer needs.

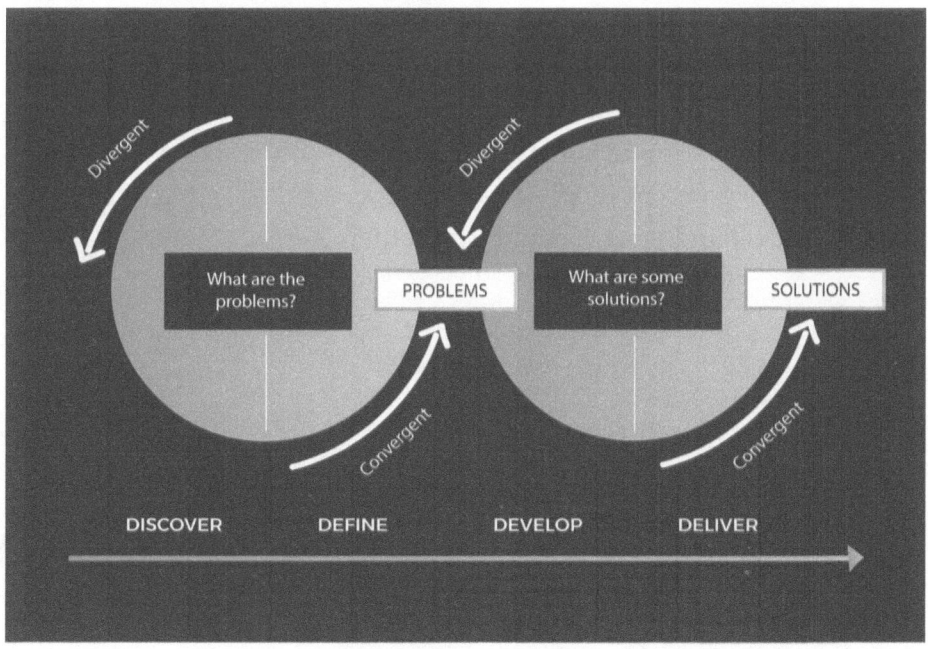

There are 4 phases to the above approach, i.e., Discover, Define, Develop and Deliver.

- **Discover** - Discover the problems that your customers are facing. Spend time with them and find out what they need.

- **Define** – Define specific problems and bucket them. Find out the essential requirements.

- **Develop** – Develop potential solutions that are feasible to solve customer problems that arise from the first diamond.

- **Deliver** – Deliver a desirable and viable product/feature and keep iterating the process. Culminate features that are not needed.

Overall, the above 4 phases lead to five steps of the design thinking process, thus, turning ideas into solutions, where each stage is iterative.

1. **Empathise**: The ability to understand and share another person's feelings from their frame of reference is called empathy. In this case, the product owners need to have divergent thinking and understand the key issues their customers are facing to the maximum extent. Explore the highest limit to identify the challenges, needs and opportunities. Conduct primary or secondary research to develop an understanding of your customers. Have focus groups, observations, customer interviews, research reports, empathy mapping, etc., to understand your customers and their needs.

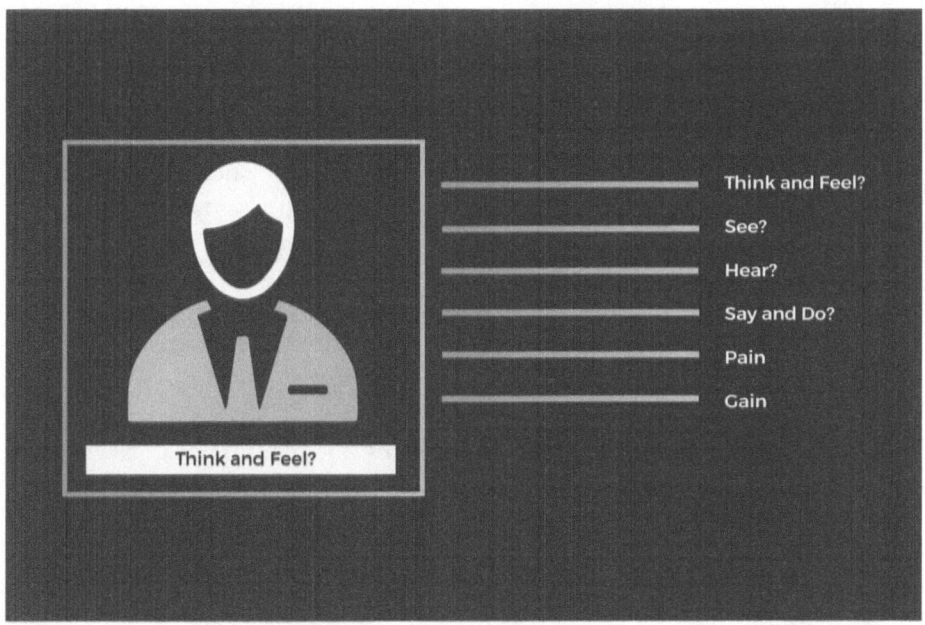

The empathy map template helps understand the point of view of product owners and application owners from a customer standpoint. Some of the key questions which should arise from this design thinking session are:

- What are the pain points of the users for the existing product?
- What does the user talk about the product on different social channels or websites?
- Are they looking for something new, which they are comparing with other service providers?
- What do you hear about your product from different people within the organization as internal users?
- What kind of users are you expecting from this product? Do they have any aspirations or are they just muddled up in existing issues?

The outcome of empathy leads to understanding different customer segments, building up personas, understanding how users react and responding under different situations when interviewed by the organization.

2. **Define**: Now, with divergent thinking and understanding empathy, multiple points would have got listed. It's now essential to apply convergent thinking and start focusing on the user's needs. Have a clear demarcation regarding their likes and dislikes. Organise all the aspects across your current user experience and find out what they need more.

3. **Ideate**: Ideation is to get more thinking around the creative ideas that have come from the 'define' stage to find solutions to the problem. Brainstorming, mind-mapping and storyboards could be viable solutions around it. Let your team go crazy in this space to get more creative ideas to fulfil user needs.

4. **Prototype**: Building a prototype is putting the idea in a defined set of frameworks that a user can understand. Wireframe/sketch creation is the best way to express these thoughts, which can be further discussed and brainstormed to get a minimum viable product (MVP). Find out which ideas you would like to pursue immediately, depending on the prioritisation framework.

5. **Test**: Take the feedback from your users. Find out whether the requirements defined from the empathy template built into the prototype solve the users' problems. Understand user behaviour and check for the average engagement time of the new service/feature introduced. If you have created two different versions of the screen, you can also go ahead with A/B testing to find out where more engagement is happening.

Remember, the above is process is iterative and needs commitment from the entire team to proceed ahead for quick design, development, testing and implementation in an agile manner. The world is changing, hence, the customer needs as well. The quicker you are in understanding the customer's need and implementing it, the more your product will be successful.

Prioritisation Frameworks

During the outcome of the double diamond approach, several ideas/feature requirements come in place. It is of utmost importance for product managers to set priorities, depending on the business need and immediate requirements. Sometimes, there are specific sets of features which we know are very important but will take more time for development. Then there are others, which will not take much time but are not that important, whereas some features might bring in revenue on an immediate basis while others will enhance the customer's experience and resolve their issues.

There are several frameworks around prioritising the product requirements and product managers need to set an explicit requirement in terms of what should go first and thereafter.

MoSCoW Model

MoSCoW method is a very well-known prioritisation technique, which is used in business analysis, product management, project management, etc., to prioritise what should go first and is of immediate need.

MoSCoW is an acronym for **Must have, Should have, Could have** and **Won't have.**

- Must have are the requirements which should immediately be taken into consideration as per the business need.

- Should have requirements are important, not urgent and should be prioritised after must have. These are also essential requirements, however, the project's success should not be dependent on them.

- Could have are the requirements which are desirable but not necessarily required. It is less critical as compared to should have and should be given priority thereafter.

- Won't have requirements are those requirements which are not needed at the current point in time, and its delivery can be prioritised for later releases. They are not invalid requirements, nevertheless, they are not needed at this point in time.

This model applies to all types of activities and is very useful in managing tasks across several departments. The DSDM (Dynamic Service Development Method) Consortium recommends a limit on the percentage of requirements that can be assigned to any one MoSCoW priority category. It advises no more than 60% in Must, 20% in Should and 20% in Could.

RICE Framework

RICE stands for **Reach, Impact, Confidence and Effort**. It is also one method of prioritising ideas and features based on the ranking assigned to the above parameters.

1. **Reach** – How many of your customers will be impacted by the new feature released? How much reach will the new feature bring in? As a product owner, you need to ensure to calculate the reach over a period; it could be a month, quarter, half-yearly or yearly (answers backed by data).

2. **Impact** - Impact refers to the set of outcomes that you are planning to achieve. The feature that will have more impact, say, for example, will reduce the number of calls at the call center, bring in more customers, generate more revenue, add value to a product and position us differently, will have a higher impact. A scaled parameter approach can be taken into consideration to measure the effect, i.e., Massive Impact – 3.0, High Impact – 2.0, Medium Impact – 1.0, Low Impact – 0.5, Minimal Impact – 0.25.

3. **Confidence** - It refers to how much confidence we have in the reach and impact. If there is data to back this up, it will give more confidence and the score will increase. However, for the one that we are going ahead with on intuition, it will lead to a decrease

in confidence score. It is measured as High Confidence – 100%, Medium Confidence – 80% and Low Confidence – 50%.

4. **Effort** – Sometimes, we know features that are of utmost importance, however, the overall effort to bring that feature in is high. You might have to get approval from multiple stakeholders and ensure all policies and procedures are met, which might take a high-end effort. Less effort will lead to a quick release. Measuring of efforts is solely based on the number of resources involved in delivering the same. It is estimated as the number of person-hours, weeks or months, depending on the overall requirement, and is estimated as the number of resources involved to complete a task over a given period.

$$\text{RICE Score} = \frac{\text{Reach} * \text{Impact} * \text{Confidence}}{\text{Effort}}$$

Feature	Reach	Impact	Confidence	Effort	RICE Score
Transaction Enquiry for chatbot	5000	2	100%	0.5	20,000
Rate enquiry feature for remittance	5000	2.5	100%	1	12,500
Remittance booking feature for chatbot	2500	3	80%	2	3,000

Value Vs Complexity

Value vs complexity refers to the business value add a feature or service will bring versus the complexity involved in implementing the same. Assess every quadrant to see which feature you want to implement first, which has a better value add from a customer/business perspective and is less complex to implement.

High Value and Low Complexity: These are the set of features and services which are less complex to implement and provide more business value to the organization. These are the ones which should be taken on priority and are easy to go.

High Value and High Complexity: These are the set of features and services that have high business value but may take more time to implement. It should be defined as a part of the product roadmap and should be further broken down into multiple milestones to move it to an easy-to-go stage.

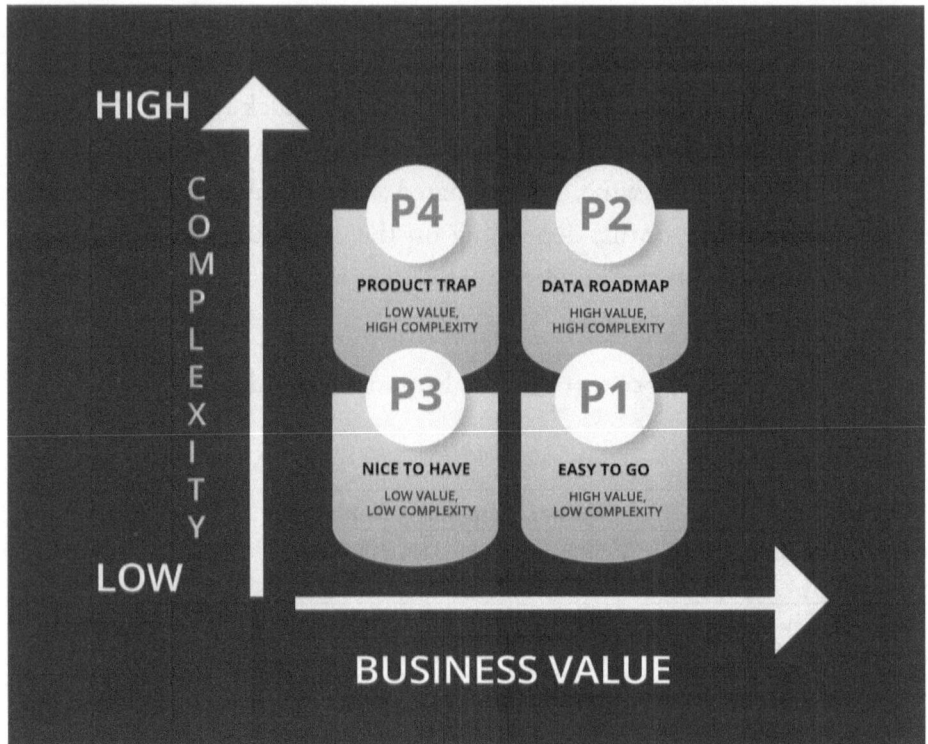

Low Value and Low Complexity: Apart from high value and low complexity, these are the services/features which the technical team would like to go to next. Though, they are easier to implement and will keep on reflecting that something is being added to the product, the value add, however, is extremely low. Customers would not pay much attention to it and as a product manager, it will be difficult to identify the KPIs. These are nice to have but should not be given immediate priority as business value is missing.

Low Value and High Complexity: These are the set of features that technically sound amazing to implement, but don't add any business value to the organization and customer. Such a set of features should be immediately dropped as they are not worth the effort to implement and are a sheer wastage of time and effort of all.

ICE Framework

The ICE framework is also one of the prioritisation methods followed by product owners, to manage the requirements' backlogs and suggest which one should go first. Though it sounds somewhat similar to RICE, however, it is different as it doesn't involve the reach factor and the effort. Let us understand this in more detail.

1. **Impact** – It refers to the effect that the feature/service/product is going to create. How much will it impact the overall users? Whether it will add benefits to the customer or make a significant impact from a business standpoint and generate more revenue. It is measured on a scale of 1-10, where 9-10 represents significant impact, 6-8 medium/definite impact, 2-5 minimal impact and 1 no impact.

2. **Confidence** – Confidence refers to the overall confidence on the impact, which has been thought. If data, customer feedback, etc., have backed the impact, it will reflect more confidence and hence, the hypothesis stands true. However, if there is more uncertainty around the impact, the confidence score tends to decrease. It is also measured on a scale of 1-10, where 1-3 represents a high risk, 4-7 medium risk and 8-10 low risk.

3. **Ease** – Ease is about the easiness to complete and launch a feature. Features which can quickly move from product backlog to release backlog/sprint backlog and then to shipment, are more preferred, as they can quickly receive feedback from customers and go for iteration, in case needed. In the case of agile execution, we can swiftly find the ease of completing a particular task. It is scaled as 1-2 for one month or more, 3-5 for one to two weeks, 6-7 for less than a week and 8-10 for less than one day.

ICE Score = Impact * Confidence* Ease

Feature	Impact	Confidence	Effort	ICE Score
Transaction Enquiry for chatbot	9	10	5	450
Rate enquiry feature for remittance	9	9	4	324
Remittance booking feature for chatbot	10	8	2	160

Kano Model

Kano model, though developed in 1980 by Noriaki Kano, is still in use to classify customer preferences. Several techniques specify customer satisfaction with product features or services. The Kano model has three types of attributes to products and services. These attributes are – Basics, Satisfiers and Delighters.

1. **Basics** – Basic features or services are the initial expectations that a customer has from a product or service. Customers will not go for the product if the basics of necessity are not met.

2. **Satisfiers** – It increases the satisfaction level of the customer. The customer might be expecting it and if received, it would bring him more satisfaction.

3. **Delighters** – Making the customer delighted is like providing features/services which the customers would have not even thought of or asked for. Nonetheless, their presence would have created a high-end wow experience.

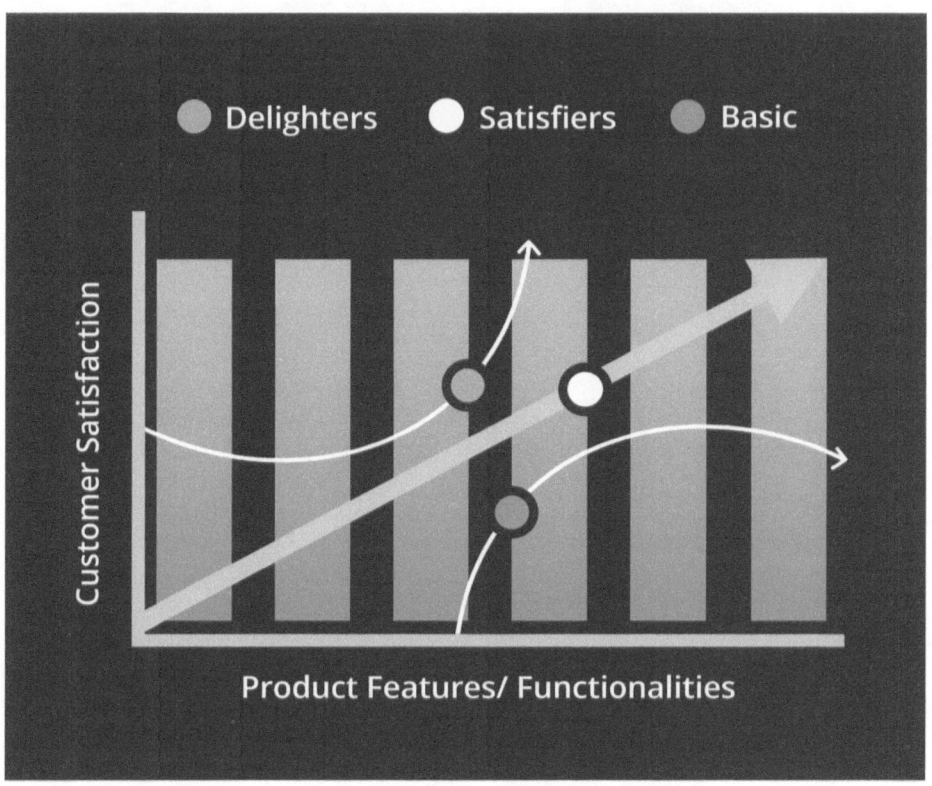

Creating Business Case

Creating a compelling story to present your idea in terms of numbers, gives a substantial endowment to get a project nod from stakeholders. However, I have seen many product managers face challenges while creating compelling business cases, and presenting them without veracious facts and figures, leading to many ideas getting rejected.

Every written document should be made keeping the end-user, who will read it, in mind and what they will infer from it. Most of the time in organizations, it is either the Finance team or the Commercial Pricing team who does this evaluation and recommends whether the project/idea presented makes business sense.

From the product owner's standpoint, a strong business case reflects a long-term strategy which has been thought around the product, and how the overall P&L of the product will perform. However, don't expect finance to approve your project if it is just a mere idea and doesn't provide any value add to your existing business.

Let's understand some of the vital processes around creating a business case and its methodologies.

- If the data is available within the organization, present your business case with the support of that data.

- Reach out to your MIS (Management Information System) team, to get the existing data that is available.

- If the data is not available, back it up with secondary research which clearly articulates how the number has arrived.

- Understand how your competitors are performing (during the benchmark analysis), and mark your assumptions against that.

- Always have a broader view while thinking around the numbers and ensure the data is accurate.

- Keep reviewing your numbers even after the project is approved, so that it indicates when you are approaching the break-even to generate profit.

- You can also consider the worst-case and best-case scenarios to support the research data.

Remember, it's not only your idea or product for the finance team. They have to make a factual decision considering the overall portfolio of investments across the organization. If the year demands fewer investments across the new product segment, however strong your business case might be, it may have a chance to be put on hold.

Therefore, it is recommended to understand your company's balance sheet and see where the overall expenses are happening. If the company has enough cash in hand and are looking for good investments, go ahead and present your idea with a strong business case to your stakeholders and get a big yes from everyone.

Financial Terminologies for Writing a Business Case

We will go through some essential financial terminologies such as NPV, IRR, Payback Period, Discounting, Opportunity Cost, ROI, etc. This is to understand, **Is the project worth investing?**

Payback Period

Payback period is the time period in which you get your invested money back. It helps in knowing within how many years the initial investment made will return. It is used by financial experts for acceptance or rejection of business proposals.

Examples:

1. Suppose a company is planning to invest 500,000 USD and the project is expected to generate 150,000 USD as net cash flow every year, for a period of 5 years. The payback period for such type of a project (**even cash flows**) would be:

    Payback period = Initial Investment/ Cash inflow for that period

    i.e. Payback period = 500,000/150,000 = 3.33 years

2. Suppose a company is planning to invest 500,000 USD and the project is generating **uneven cash flows** for a 5 year time period as mentioned below:

    Payback period = A + B/C, where

    A is the last year which has negative cumulative cash flow;

    B is the absolute value of the cumulative cash flow of Year A;

    C is the total cash flow during the year after Year A.

	Year 0	Year 1	Year 2	Year 3	Year 4	Year 5
Investment						
Partner1 Cost	$ (30,000.00)					
Partner2 Cost	$ (40,000.00)					
Software Development Cost	$ (100,000.00)					
Hardware Cost	$ (200,000.00)					
Integration Cost	$ (130,000.00)					
Total Expense	$ (500,000.00)					
Total Cashflow	$ (500,000.00)	75,000	100,000	150,000	200,000	220,000
Cumulative cash flow	$ (500,000.00)	$ (425,000.00)	$ (325,000.00)	$ (175,000.00)	$ 25,000.00	$ 245,000.00

- A is the 3rd year
- B is 175,000
- C is 200,000

Therefore, Payback period = 3rd Year + 175,000/200,000 = 3.87 Years

There can be another scenario, wherein the investment is ongoing for specific years - say Year 1 and Year 2. The project is generating an **uneven cash flows** for a 5 year time period, as mentioned above. In such scenarios, the total cash flow will differ, and the expenses will be subtracted from the income to calculate the net cash flow. The rest of the process remains the same.

Time Value of Money

Time value of money is the concept where the value of money increases compared to its present value. It is as simple as, say you hold 1000 USD in your savings account and earn a 10% interest for a year. The amount of money next year will be 1100 USD. The payback period doesn't include the time value of money, and hence, it is not considered an accurate tool for measurement.

Present Value

The present value of money is defined as the current value of money w.r.t. the amount received at a future date. It includes the time value of money.

$PV = FV/ (1+i)^n$ Where

- PV is present value;
- FV is future value;
- i is rate of interest;
- n is number of years

Suppose you would be receiving, say, 1000 USD after a 5 year time period, with an interest rate of 10%. The present value of the amount will be:

$PV = 1000/ (1+0.1)^5 = 1000/ (1.1)^5 = 620.92$

Net Present Value

Net present value is calculated as the difference between the present value of all future cash inflows with the present value of cash outflows. It determines if it is worth investing in a project.

The formula used for calculation is-

$$NPV = -C_0 + \frac{C_1}{1+r} + \frac{C_2}{(1+r)^2} + ... + \frac{C_T}{(1+r)^T}$$

- $-C_0 = Initial\ Investment$
- $C = Cash\ Flow$
- $r = Discount\ Rate$
- $T = Time$

You can also use an excel formula to find the NPV. There is a function called **NPV,** which can be used for the same. However, you have to subtract the initial investment from it.

Let us consider a similar example as discussed in payback period example 2, where the discount rate was been taken as 10%.

	Year 0	Year 1	Year 2	Year 3	Year 4	Year 5
Investment						
Partner1 Cost	$ (30,000.00)					
Partner2 Cost	$ (40,000.00)					
Software Development Cost	$ (100,000.00)					
Hardware Cost	$ (200,000.00)					
Integration Cost	$ (130,000.00)					
Total Cashflow	$ (500,000.00)	75,000	100,000	150,000	200,000	220,000
PV of Cash Flows	$ (500,000.00)	68,182	82,645	112,697	136,603	136,603
NPV	$ 36,729.05					

The NPV comes out to be 36,729 USD.

If the NPV of the project is negative, it is not considered to be a good investment and if the NPV of the project is higher, it is beneficial for the organization.

Discount Rate

The discount rate is the rate that is used to determine the present value of future cash flows. It is generally set by the corporate finance team and is the cost of borrowing money or the rate of return, which is expected by the investors. From an organization standpoint, it is often referred to as the hurdle rate, the required rate of return or the weighted average cost of capital (WACC).

WACC is calculated as:

$$WACC = \frac{E}{V} \times R_e + \frac{D}{V} \times R_d \times (1-T_c)$$

Where

E = market value of total equity;

D = market value of total debt;

V = total value of financing i.e. D+E;

Re = Cost of equity;

Rd = Cost of debt;

T = Tax rate

WACC is an important metric from an organization standpoint, as it signifies whether it is worth investing in the company or not. If a company has a higher WACC, it means the overall cost of financing has been higher for the firm.

Internal Rate of Return

The internal rate of return is the interest rate at which the Net Present Value (NPV) is zero. It should be higher than the cost of funds, else, it is not recommended to proceed with the project. If IRR > discount rate, NPV will be >0, if IRR < discount rate, NPV will be <0 and if IRR = discount rate, NPV = 0.

For example, taking the above data as mentioned in the NPV table, if we calculate IRR, it will be 12%. Use the excel formula and do the IRR function around total cash outflows and inflows.

ATAR Business Model

ATAR is a forecasting business model that stands for Awareness, Trial, Availability and Repeat. The marketing team and product team also use it to forecast business revenue, profits, volumes or imminent marketing campaigns.

Universe: It is the target market segment or the market potential of the products and services being offered.

Awareness: It is about how many users are aware of you as a brand or how many of your customers are aware of what you do. It could be your existing customers from multiple channels or could also be the percentage of customers you want to target to create awareness, from the market size. It is defined as the total number of people who are aware of your products and services.

Trial: It refers to the number of people who will or want to try your product and services.

Availability: It refers to the reach of your products and services to the consumers. If the accessibility of the store is 24*7 and it is nearby, then the reach is high. For example, all the digital channel services have 100% reach, as they are not time-bounded. However, in the case of brick and mortar, the reach percentage differs depending on the store's availability.

Repeat (Retrial): Refers to the number of customers who will repeatedly use your products and services w.r.t their satisfaction from the initial buying.

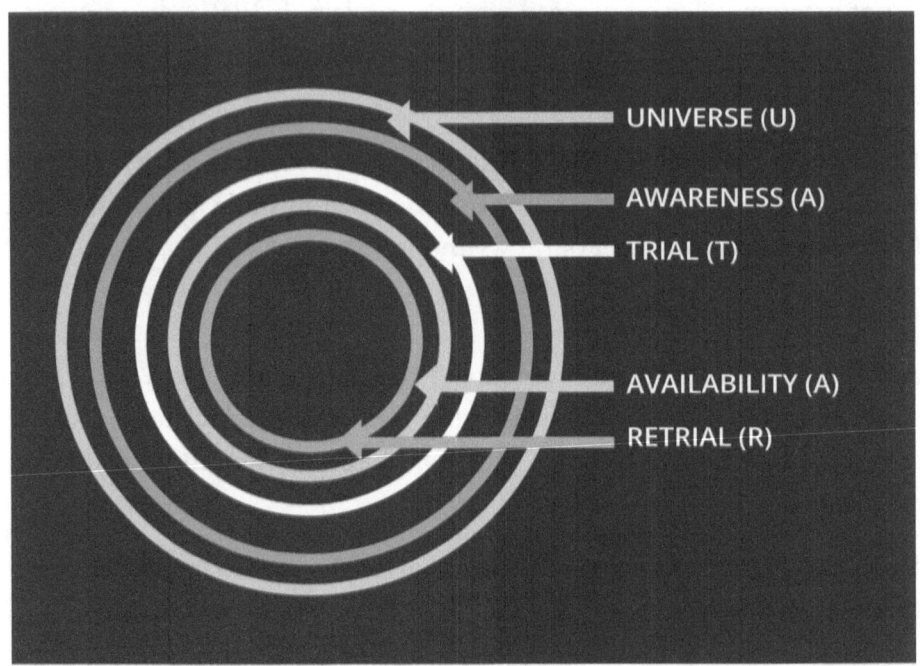

ATAR model applies to several sets of products and services provided by the firm to the consumers. Products that are purchased by customers on an annual basis will be 100% or the multiple of 1 while the product that is replaced every six months, will have a multiple of 8.

Note: For the excel template, kindly refer to marketingstudyguide.com, which can be used as per the business model need.

Business Model Canvas

Business Model Canvas is a strategic management tool designed by Alex Osterwalder, which can be used to develop new or document existing business models. It contains nine components – Key Partners, Key Activities, Key Resources, Value Proposition, Customer Relationships, Customer Segments, Channels along with two additional sections to document your

Cost Structure and Revenue Streams. It is one of the crucial strategic tools to breakdown the various elements that make the business work.

Let us understand each and every element associated with the business model, which needs to be used to create a useful business model.

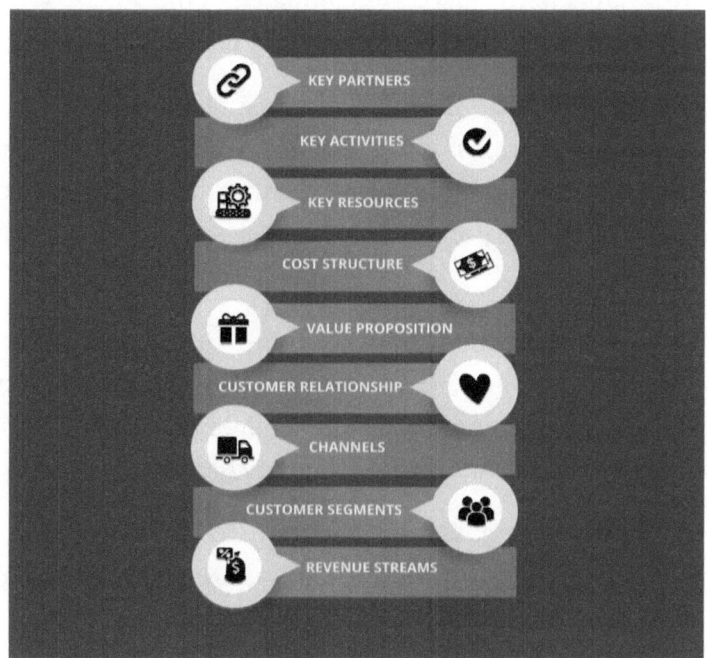

1. **Key Partners**: Key partners are the companies or organizations with whom we need to enter into a strategic partnership to provide value-added services to our customers. What are the resources which we would need from those partners?

2. **Key Activities:** Activities that we need to perform to deliver value to our customers. Do we need to do market research? Do we need to develop new products and services? Do we need to engage with our customers with marketing efforts?

3. **Key Resources**: Resources which are required to deliver value to our customers. They could be tangible or intangible resources,

i.e., tangible resources such as tools, materials, etc., and intangible resources such as distribution channels, technology, etc.

4. **Value Proposition**: Value proposition refers to the benefits that are being provided to the customer. How are we differentiating the product in the market as compared to the others? Why will the user use this product? What problem of the user is being solved?

5. **Customer Relationships**: Customer relationship is focused on the kind of relationship we need to maintain with our customers. It refers to the relationship we want to have with our customers and what they expect from us as consumers of our products and services.

6. **Channels**: Channels refer to how interaction is happening with the customers. It mentions about the most effective way of delivering the products and services while maintaining cost-effective interactions across different channels.

7. **Customer Segments**: Segmentation here refers to the different personas of the customers, whom we are targeting. What are the traits of each persona, and what products and services are they seeking?

8. **Cost Structure**: It refers to the cost of acquiring the customer.

9. **Revenue Streams**: Revenue streams refer to different ways in which charges can be levied on customers. It largely depends on the firm's customer segments and the persona's behavioural characteristics linked to that segment. It is essential to know your customer's persona because their needs and preferences are different, and may impact the overall business areas.

Build a Brand

One of the essential pillars of a product is brand-building, which plays a vital role in product development, product launch and even post that. Many stakeholders might see the brands as just visuals, colours, logos, websites, etc., however, those are just artefacts or touchpoints. The fundamental role that a brand plays is more than that, which is connecting with the audience.

Jeff Bezos, the CEO of Amazon, said it well.

> "Your brand is what people say about you when you are not in the room"

— **Jeff Bezos.**

"**make.believe**," which is the Sony brand group's message, symbolises the spirit of the brand and stands for creativity; their ability to turn ideas into reality and the belief that anything which can be imagined, can be made real. "make.believe" unites the communication efforts, thus, providing a single face to convey Sony's role to the world. It reignites the brand and inspires people about the magic of Sony. Sony says that the dot, which links make and believe, is the place where imagination and reality collide. It is the point of ignition that transcends reality. The dot is the role of Sony.

The "make.believe" mantra is the one that connects with the audience; if it's about innovation, it's Sony. They believe that:

- Curiosity is the key to creativity.
- Anything you can imagine, you can make real.

Brand Segmentation

When a brand is created, it is not targeted towards all sets of audiences. An organization knows which segment has been taken into consideration for the product/sub-product under the brand. Every product or sub-product can become a brand if the value proposition and consumer segment are explicitly identified. What revolves around the brand is the consumer and the segment. Therefore, identifying the consumers, their needs, the relevance, their choices, likes and dislikes will make a brand create an emotional connection.

Brand segmentation involves grouping or dividing the audience into sub-groups, based on common traits to optimise the marketing, advertising and sales efforts. There are four types of segmentation, i.e., Demographic, Psychographic, Behavioural and Geographic.

Demographic Segmentation: It includes components such as age, gender, income, location, education, ethnicity, socioeconomic status, etc.

Behavioural Segmentation: It talks about how an individual interacts with a brand. Do they prefer to be associated all the time or do they want to interact during specific periods? How frequently they interact with a brand, their purchasing, loyalty and spending habits, etc. It depicts the customer's action and reaction.

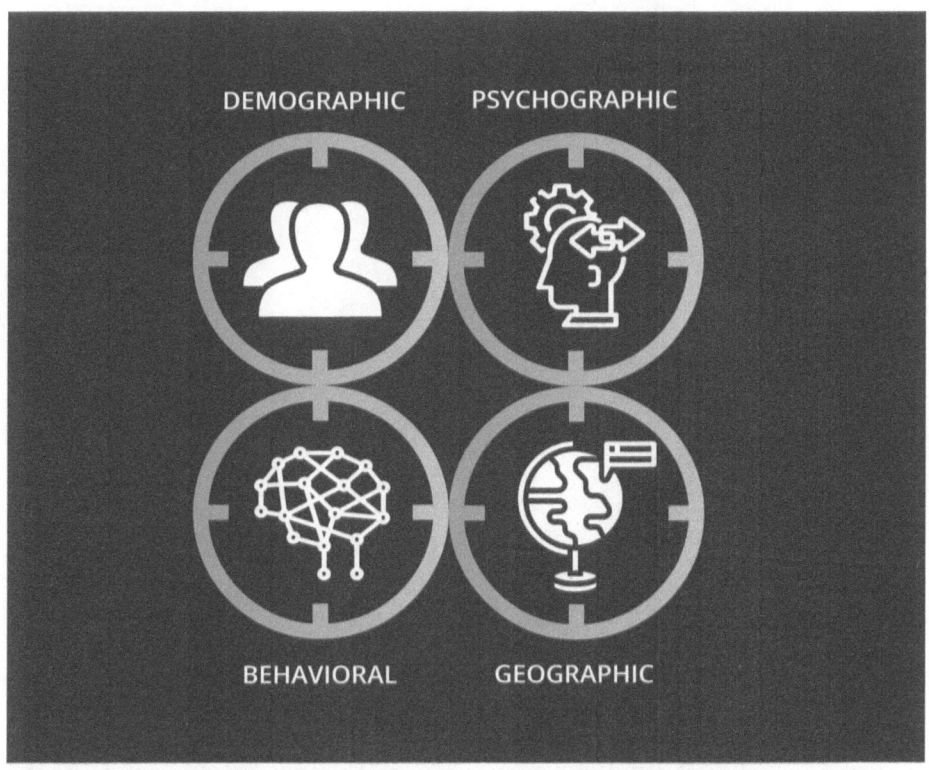

Geographic Segmentation: It is about segmenting customers apropos their geographical borders. It includes country, city, climate, urban or rural, as the target market may differ from country to country or within a country from one province to another, as the adoption patterns are different.

Psychographic Segmentation: It is one of the most important and subjective segmentations that reflects the values, attitudes, traits, motivations, priorities, lifestyles, interests, etc. This segmentation assists in knowing different personality types and essential traits that the target customer possesses.

We get to know the grouping of customers and how each segmentation depicts the consumer's purchase pattern and buying behaviour from segmentation. However, creating a customer persona helps understand the customer better as well as identify individual needs as to why they would want to buy this product, what else they are looking for, what motivates them to come here and why they value us.

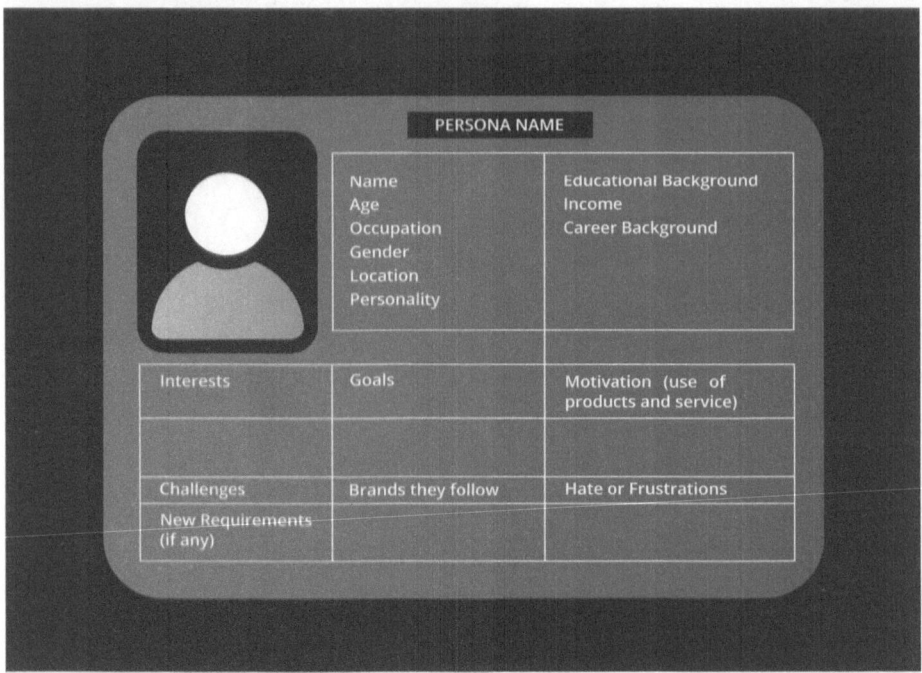

When a successful person, product or brand outshines in their career, we might see the same outside. However, the significant efforts that have gone to achieve the same lies underneath, which is not visible and needs exploration. Ernest Hemingway, an American journalist, coined the term **"Iceberg Theory"** or **"Theory of Omission"**, which suggests that we cannot see or detect most of the story beneath, nevertheless, it needs to be searched for detailed understanding.

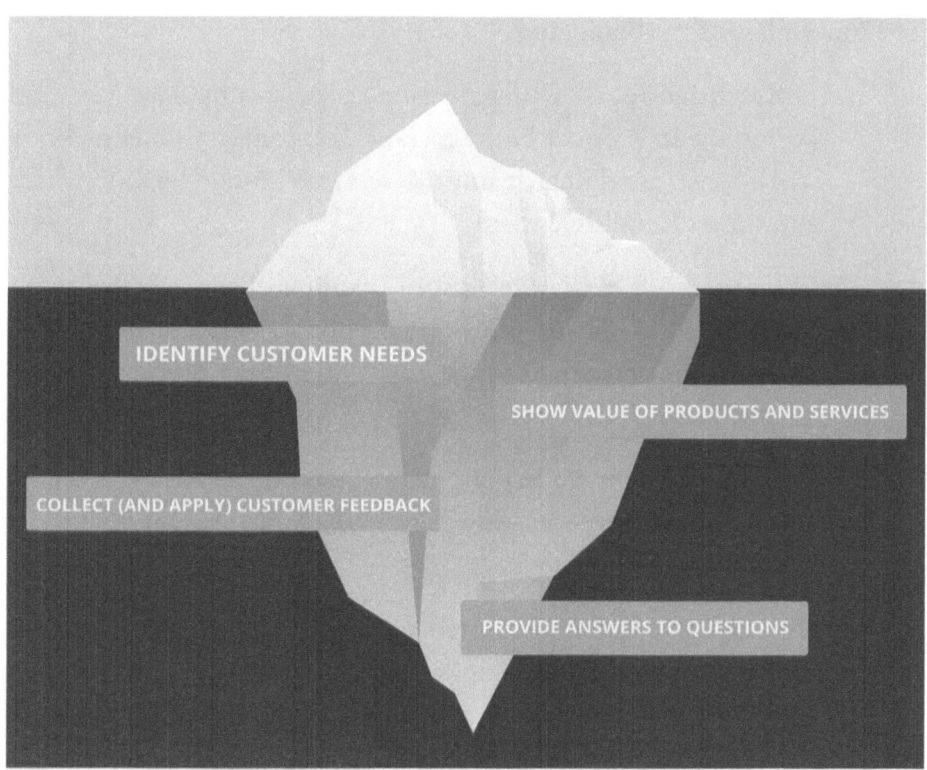

The tip of the iceberg, which is the smallest part, is visible, i.e., around 10% while the remaining 90% is underneath. This principle of the Iceberg Theory is applicable in all aspects and can be used across any department or section to identify the unanswered questions, bringing the real facts and figures in place. To understand your customers, it is of utmost importance that you recognise their pain-points, challenges, frustrations, motivations, etc. Once identified, the right solution is visible because it is based on the exact need that the consumers would have been looking for.

Brand pillars have four components that capture the well-being of forming a brand. The brand connects to the outside world through marketing communication, therefore, the connection should depict what you want to say and should bind with the customer's feelings, imagination and thoughts.

The four pillars of the brand are:

1. **Differentiation** – Differentiation is how uniquely you can position your product in the market. You cannot simply replicate what others are doing. It must have some unique features which consumers can differentiate.

2. **Relevance** – Even if the feature is unique but not relevant or meaningful, it adds no value to the entire product or brand. You will miss the context to connect with the audience since it is not relevant.

3. **Esteem** – Customers respond with esteem if the brand associates with them. Involve the customers, make them feel unique so that they remember you always.

4. **Knowledge** – Customers need to understand what the brand is trying to convey. If they understand the message, it will have a positive impact, else the adverse. Spread the right knowledge of the brand through the right message

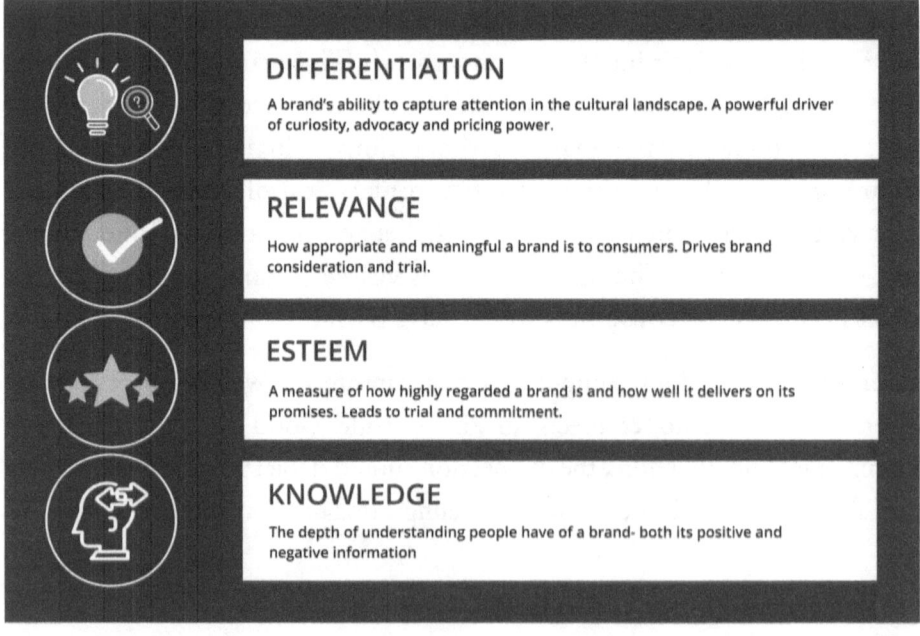

Brand Positioning

Brand positioning is referred as the organization's approach to position its brand to the end customers and enter into the consumers' minds. It is different from a tagline; a tagline is an external statement applied in marketing efforts. Positioning, however, is internal to the organization, which defines how the brand uniquely positions itself.

Simon Sinek, author of "Why: How Great Leaders Inspire Everyone to Take Action and Leaders Eat Last", mentioned that your **brand should be a relationship**, not a one-night stand. Several key elements need to be considered when doing brand positioning and creating a strong relationship with the customers, such as:

1. **Target Segment** – Who are you going to interact with? Identify what is hidden underneath the Iceberg.

2. **Frame of Reference** – The brand's frame of reference is the perspective in which consumers interpret it and the category they want to compete in. It is the foundation of the positioning, thus, determining the points of parity that a brand has to meet. The growth should not be limited by the frame of reference.

3. **Point of Difference** – What makes us think of a unique and value-based positioning? How do I differentiate the brand from its competitors?

4. **Efficacy of the brand** – Why will consumers consider you as a brand? The reasons to make them believe - "What you say is, What you do."

Let's consider the example of "**Edison international**", one of the leading firms, having 130 plus years of presence is transforming the energy industry.

The company is well-positioned and prepared for the work that lies ahead. They focus on clean energy opportunities, efficient electrification, the grid of the future, and customer choice to strengthen and grow their business.

Brand Introduction – Every day, the needs of our customers and communities evolve. New opportunities for serving them arrive. That's why we are looking ahead. We are thinking differently about who we are and what we do. The purpose of a 'brand' is to give ourselves and our customers a fresh way of looking at us today while remaining true to the same values that have sustained us throughout our history.

Employees will tell the Edison story of today. Over time, you will hear each other's stories about how we deliver value to our customers and communities. We ask that you embrace our Edison story. Be our Edison story. Bring it to life. We hope that it inspires you and gives you energy for what's ahead.

Brand Story for Edison International - Brand is much more than a tagline or a logo. It's the promise we make to our customers. It tells us who we need to be for our customers, communities and each other as we work to drive our business forward. Brand unifies us.

Brand Tagline - Our tagline is both a rallying cry for employees and the expression of the promise we make to our customers. It's how we summarise our brand story for all our audiences. Energy for What's Ahead® highlights our ongoing commitment to doing the hard work of safely delivering reliable, affordable and clean energy every day. Most importantly, it says we're going beyond every day to bring cleaner energy to a changing world.

Brand House – Through their brand house, they articulate what they aspire to be for their consumers and how they resonate with it. It reflects how Edison Energy is bringing the goals and objectives to connect with their consumers.

Build a Brand | 81

BRAND TAGLINE

Energy of what's Ahead

BRAND PURPOSE

To be the foundation for energy progress that better serves our customers, communities and environment.

BRAND DIFFERENTIATORS

HONORING OUR COMMITMENT	EMBRACING THE NEW	LEADING BY DOING	GOING THE EXTRA MILE
Safely delivering the reliable, affordable and clean energy that Southern California needs to thrive.	Supporting and enabling new energy solutions that meet the diverse needs of our customers.	Driving progress in energy efficiency and clean power for a healthier environment.	Delivering helpful services and friendly support to the communities we have lived in and served for over 130 years.

BRAND PERSONALITY

CARING	RESPONSIVE	EXPERT	VISIONARY
We own our responsibilities to our customers and communities and commit, on a human level, to the people we work with and serve.	We listen to our customers and continuously adapt to provide solutions that better serve them.	We leverage our expertise and insight to develop new technologies and facilitate progress with our partners.	We create a smarter energy infrastructure that supports our vision for a clearer environment and greater customer environment.

CULTURE	COMMUNICATIONS	CUSTOMER EXPERIENCE

References

The mentioned list of references is provided to extend your knowledge of Product Development, Management and Strategy.

Magic of Numbers

- Annis, Jim. "Why job seekers, other employees should look at financial statements." Johnson, Celeste, Miller, Tom and Chennault, Suzanne. Reno Gazette Journal (Part of the USA today network). March 11, 2014. www.rgj.com/story/money/business/2014/03/11/why-job-seekers-other-employees-should-look-at-financial-statements/6318229/

- "Financial Statement - Beginners' Guide", U.S. Securities And Exchange Commission, February 5, 2007. www.sec.gov/reportspubs/investorpublications/investorpubsbegfinstmtguidehtm.html

- Dumay, John. "Beyond Accounting for Old Wine in New Bottles." European Conference on Intangibles and Intellectual Capital, Academic Conferences International Limited, April 2017, p. 88.

- "Trademark Accounting: Everything You Need to Know.", upcounsel, www.upcounsel.com/trademark-accounting

- "The End of Accounting.", Prisim Business Simulations. www.prisim.com/wp-content/uploads/2016/07/The-End-of-Accounting-The-WSJ.pdf

- Gupta, Abhishek. "Annual Report Card FY 2019.", Oyorooms, February 17, 2020

84 | References

- "U.S. investment rates, 1977 to 2017." – Intan-Invest, http://www.intaninvest.net/charts-and-tables/

- O'Brien, Sara Ashley. "Uber says it lost $1.8 billion in 2018.", CNN Edition, February 15, 2019. www.edition.cnn.com/2019/02/15/tech/uber-2018-financial-report/index.html

- Huckabee Thomas. "Do Financial Statements Really Work for Digital Technology Startup Corporations?", Thomas Huckabee Inc., June 24, 2019. https://tehcpa.net/accounting-methods/do-financial-statements-really-work-for-digital-technology-startup-corporations/

- Zarzycki, Nick. "Understanding an Income Statement.", Bench, Reviewed by Janet Berry-Johnson, CPA on November 27, 2019. https://bench.co/blog/accounting/income-statement/

- Recommended financial analyst certifications from – "WallStreetMojo" or "CorporateFinanceInstitute"

Privacy Really Matters

- Information Commissioner's Office. "Intention to fine Marriott International Inc, more than £99 million under GDPR for data breach." July 9, 2019. Licensed under the Open Government License.

- https://ico.org.uk/about-the-ico/news-and-events/news-and-blogs/2019/07/statement-intention-to-fine-marriott-international-inc-more-than-99-million-under-gdpr-for-data-breach/

- Hughes, Emma. "Time to take notice: ICO to impose record fine for data security breach." Hogan Lovells, July 8, 2019.

- O'Flaherty, Kate. "Marriott Faces $123 Million Fine For 2018 Mega-Breach.", Forbes, July 9, 2019.

- Sundaram, Aurobindo. "UK Information Commissioner's Office intends to fine British Airways £183.39M - Industry Implications.", LinkedIn.com, July 15, 2019.

- Corfield, Gareth. "UK data watchdog kicks £280m British Airways and Marriott GDPR fines into legal long grass.", www.theregister.com, Jan 13, 2020

- Information Commissioner's Office. "International airline fined £500,000 for failing to secure its customers' personal data." March 4, 2020. Licensed under the Open Government License.

- https://ico.org.uk/about-the-ico/news-and-events/news-and-blogs/2020/03/international-airline-fined-500-000-for-failing-to-secure-its-customers-personal-data/

- Information Commissioner's Office. "What is a DPIA", ICO. Licensed under the Open Government License.

- https://ico.org.uk/for-organisations/guide-to-data-protection/guide-to-the-general-data-protection-regulation-gdpr/data-protection-impact-assessments-dpias/what-is-a-dpia/

- Brook, Chris. "Data Controller vs. Data Processor. What's The Difference?" Digital Guardian, Jan 8, 2020

- "GDPR Compliance Statement." Evisort, May 2020

- "The 10 Privacy Principles of PIPEDA.", Privacy Sense, www.privacysense.net

- McCreary, Mark G. "Tackling Privacy by Design: Practical Advice Following Multiple Implementations", CPO Magazine May 21, 2020.

- Blum, Dan. "Privacy By Design And The Online Library Environment." Information Standards Quarterly, vol. 26, no. 3, National Information Standards Organization, Oct. 2014, p. 4.

- "Principles relating to processing of personal data.", Intersoft Consulting, www.gdpr.eu
- Wolford Ben, "A guide to GDPR data privacy requirements.", GDPR.EU
- Cavoukian, Ann Ph.D., "Privacy by Design.", Information & Privacy Commissioner Ontario, Canada, International association of privacy professionals, www.iapp.org
- Guy, Privacy. "7 Principles of Privacy By Design." www.medium.com, Nov 20, 2017
- Bhatia, Puneet. "Data subject rights according to GDPR.", EU GDPR Academy
- "What personal data is considered sensitive?", European Commission

Thinking Strategically

- Hussain A. Ali Mahdi, "International Journal of Business Management and Economic Research, Vol 6(3), 2015,167-177
- Nickols Fred, Managing Partner of Distance Consulting, "Three Forms of Strategy", 2016
- Holusha John, " Click: Up, Down and Out at Kodak", The New York Times, https://www.nytimes.com/1989/12/09/business/click-up-down-and-out-at-kodak.html, Dec 9, 1989
- Porter Michael, "Competitive Advantage: Creating and Sustaining Superior Performance"
- Flipkart Mission, Vision and Values, www.comparably.com
- Mui Chunka, "How Kodak Failed" www.forbes.com, Jan 18, 2012

- Innolytics – Exploring Future Markets, Innovation management and idea management software's

- Kodak from bluechip to bankrupt, www.youtube.com

- Stempel Jonathan, "Kodak loses patent case vs. Apple, RIM; plans appeal", Reuters, Jul 22, 2012

- Fernando A. P. Gimenez, "Miles and Snow's strategy model in the context of small firms"

- Miles, Raymond E., and Charles C. Snow. Organizational Strategy, Structure, and Process. New York: McGraw-Hill, 1978

- Mind Tools, Porter's Generic Strategy – Choosing root to success

Building the Right Product

- MoSCoW Prioritization, www.bawiki.com

- RICE Template & Example for Teams | Miro. https://miro.com/templates/rice/

- Design Thinking – www.ideou.com

- Product Discovery – Romanpichler, Productboard, ProductPlan, ProductTalk, Productcraft (Recommended read for product user's)

- Heffernan J Kayla, Medium.com, Design Thinking 101 — The Double Diamond Approach (Part II of II), May 8, 2017

- Nielsen Norman Group – World Leaders in Research Based User Experience, www.nngroup.com

- Kelly David, "Eight design capabilities of creative problem solvers", www.ideou.com

- Hygger – The Kanban tool for software development

Creating Business Case

- Course Hero, "Payback Period"
- Corporate Finance Institute, "Financial Analyst Certifications"
- My Accounting Course, "The Easy Way to Learn Accounting"
- Harrigan Kelly, "How many people will adopt your product", August 4, 2020
- ATAR Formula, "How the ATAR Forecasting Model Works", Marketing Study Guide.com
- Startupyapper, "ATAR – Why you should focus on this for Customer Acquisition", startupyapper.wordpress.com
- Business Model Canvas Template - A Guide to Business Planning. https://corporatefinanceinstitute.com/resources/knowledge/strategy/business-model-canvas-template/
- Business Model Canvas, "Slidemodel.com"

Build a Brand

- The Iceberg Analogy of Stuttering, http://istuttersowhat.com/the-iceberg-analogy-of-stuttering/
- Edison Brand Central. https://www.edisonbrandcentral.com/
- Gilliland Nikki, "What are customer personas and why are they so important?" August 9, 2017
- Michael, Brand Positioning Basics: Establishing The Competitive Frame of Reference, Branduniq, October 22, 2015
- Tow Hannah, "What Is Market Segmentation? How to Use It for Max ROI", Learning Hub, June 10, 2020
- Irwin Terry, "The four pillars of branding", TCii Strategic and Management Consultants, July 15, 2011

www.ingramcontent.com/pod-product-compliance
Lightning Source LLC
Chambersburg PA
CBHW020928180526
45163CB00007B/2935